St.Joachim, Fort Auguste (Fort Edmonton)

Baptisms, Marriages and Burials

1858-1890

Gail Morin

Second Edition 2016

...., Albert: B-64, Albert, baptized 2 March 1861, age 10 months, parents unknown, Alb. Lacombe priest o.m.i. (page 31)

...., Alexandre: B-45, Alexandre, baptized 8 October 1859, age 3 months, illegitimate son of Otayamiwis, Godmother: Rosalie L'hyrondelle, C. M. Frain o.m.i. (page 17)

...., Alexis: B-10, Alexis (illegitimate), baptized 24 July 1886, age 2 months, son of Bella and unknown, Godmother: Nancy Hamelin, H. Grandin o.m.i. (page 112)

...., Ambroise: B-19, Ambroise, baptized 5 October 1885, age about 22 years, Godfather: Ambroise Gray, H. Grandin o.m.i. (page 108)

...., Angele: B-11, Angele, baptized 7 August 1887, born 24 July 1887, daughter of Isidore __ and Susanne Tyato, Godfather: George Ward, Godmother: Awieksiw, Tissier priest o.m.i. (page 120)

...., Anne (Marie): B-3, Anne (Marie), baptized 5 March 1884, age 35, a protestant, H. Grandin. (page 97)

...., Annie: B-21, Annie, baptized 11 October 1885, age one month, daughter of Thomas and Marie, Godmother: Eliza Shields, H. Grandin o.m.i. (page 108)

...., Antoine: B-15, Antoine, baptized 25 May 1883, age 2 months, son of Marianne Maurisaw, father unknown, Godfather: Antoine Pacquette, Godmother: Sophie, his wife, C. Scollen priest o.m.i. (page 90)

...., Betsey: B-123, Betsey, baptized 1 February 1863, age 10 days, illegitimate daughter of Marie Kizewatsiwop, Godmother: Lisette Gladu, Alb. Lacombe priest o.m.i. (page 46)

...., Catherine: B-20, Catherine, baptized 11 October 1885, age about 30 years, Godfather: Bernard _, Godmother: Julia, wife Kowllau, H. Grandin o.m.i. (page 108)

...., Isabelle: B-9, Isabelle, baptized 26 January 1871, age 4 years, Godmother: Isabelle Bruno, V. Bourgine priest. (page 73)

...., Isabelle: B-10, Isabelle, baptized 26 January 1871, Godmother: Isabelle Bruno, V. Bourgine priest. (page 73)

...., Jean Baptiste: B-28, Jean Baptiste, baptized 7 May 1859, previously baptized a Protestant, age 2 years, son of Kiwebinisk, Godfather: Baptiste Courtepatte, C. M. Frain m.o.m.i. (page 13)

...., Jean Baptiste: B-59, Jean Baptiste, baptized 27 February 1861, age 3 months, son of Pippakwat and Ohlistahek, Godfather: Jean Marie Boucher, Alb. Lacombe priest o.m.i. (page 30-31)

...., Jean-Baptiste: B-1, Jean-Baptiste, baptized 1 January 1886, born 6 December 1885, of Charles and Sarah, Godmother: Josephte, H. Grandin o.m.i. (page 110)

...., Jean Baptiste: B-16, Jean Baptiste, baptized 12 November 1887, age 3 months, of Mawitoneyichiyan (infidel) and an unknown father, Godmother: Tarepk, H. Grandin o.m.i. (page 121-122)

...., Jean Baptiste: B-4, Jean Baptiste, baptized 10 March 1884, age 2 years, son of Norbert and Elizabeth, Godfather: Louis, H. Grandin. (page 97)

...., Jean Baptiste: B-8, Jean Baptiste (illegitimate), baptized 11 May 1884, age 5 weeks, son of Julie Wetakweklukkaniw, Godmother: Catherine Ep..., H. Grandin priest o.m.i. (page 98)

...., Joseph: B-15, Joseph, baptized 22 September 1872, age one year, of Chapomanikka and Nepistchaski, infidels, Godfather: Pierre Lebrun, Blanchey priest o.m.i. (page 79)

...., Joseph: B-18, Joseph, baptized 27 September 1885, age one month, son of Jane and father unknown, Godmother: Annie Foley, H. Grandin o.m.i. (page 107)

...., Joseph: B-5, Joseph (illegitimate), baptized 23 March 1884, son of Papatiskwew, H. Grandin. (page 97)

...., Joseph: B-6, Joseph (illegitimate), baptized 27 March 1884, son of Marie Wapikakwa Crise H. Grandin. (page 97)

...., Josephine: B-11, Josephine, baptized 17 June 1888, age 6 days, of Maggy Jacob, Godmother: Nancy M..., H. Grandin o.m.i. (page 125)

...., Julie: B-13, Julie, baptized 22 August 1884, age 3 months, daughter of Senakew and Josephte, Godfather: Norman Vandale, H. Grandin o.m.i. (page 100)

...., Julienne: B-5, Julienne, baptized 8 June 1860, age one month, parents unknown, Godmother: Philomene Shalifoux, Albert Lacombe priest o.m.i. (page 19-20)

...., Magdeleine: B-144, Magdeleine, baptized 15 March 1863, age over one month, daughter of William and Marie, Godmother: Rosalie L'hyrondelle, J. M. H. Caer o.m.i. (page 50)

...., Marguerite: B-14, Marguerite, baptized 22 September 1872, age 3 years, of Kwakarcumakan and Otakkwekawni, infidels, Godfather: Pierre Lebrun, Blanchey priest o.m.i. (page 79)

...., Marguerite: B-3, Marguerite, baptized 11 May 1874, age 2 months, daughter of Jeanny, Godmother: Peggy, wife of Charles Gautier, J. Joseph Dupuis priest o.m.i. (page 83)

...., Marie: B-44, Marie, baptized 24 February 1861, age 80 years, Godfather: Catherine Cardinal, Alb. Lacombe priest o.m.i. (page 28)

...., Marie: B-4, Marie, baptized 24 January 1871, born __, of the marriage of Antoine __ and Elise __, Godmother: __, V. Bourgine priest. (page 72)

...., Marie: B-8, Marie, baptized 26 January 1871, born yesterday, of the marriage of ___, Godfather: Joseph Vendale, Godmother: Marie Todd, V. Bourgine priest. (page 73)

...., Marie: B-13, Marie, baptized 22 September 1872, age 3 months, of Akkamarcia and Pitchikkimissatappcakki, infidels, Godfather: Pierre Lebrun, Blanchey priest o.m.i. (page 79)

...., Marie: B-2, Marie, baptized 10 May 1873, daughter of Nabasis ... Kawiyowit and Catherine Kakatchik, Godfather: Henri Paquet, Godmother: Cecile his wife, J. Joseph Dupuis priest o.m.i. (page 80)

...., Marie: B-20, Marie, baptized 28 December 1884, age 2 months, daughter of Telen and Michikawe, Godmother: Marie wife of Norris, H. Grandin priest o.m.i. (page 101)

...., Marie: B-9, Marie ..., baptized 10 July 1874, age 5 months, daughter of ... and Marie Plante, Godfather: ... Brunet, Godmother: ..., .. priest. (page 84)

...., Nancy: B-3, Nancy, baptized 10 May 1873, age 6 years, orphan, Godfather: Henri Pasquet, Jr., Godmother: Philomene Pasquet, J. Joseph Dupuis priest o.m.i. (page 80)

...., Paul: B-9, Paul, baptized 2 June 1887, age 2 years, son of Cecile and an unknown father, Godfather: Rev. A. Therien, H. Grandin o.m.i. (page 120)

...., Paul: B-13, Paul, baptized 14 August 1887, age 10 years, son of John M... and Annie, Godfather: .. Thiriault, H. Grandin o.m.i. (page 120-121)

...., Suzanne: B-1, Suzanne [...], baptized ... February 1873, daughter of Paul ... and Susette Colatiskewes, Godfather: Norbert Larence, J. Joseph Dupuis priest o.m.i. (page 80)

...., Suzanne: B-4, Suzanne, baptized 8 March 1885, age 18 days, daughter of La Louise Takwesis, Godfather: David Dagneau, Godmother: Marie wife of Norris, H. Grandin o.m.i. (page 104)

Akiskow, Daniel: B-4, Daniel Akiskow, baptized 3 April 1887, age 3 years, son of Akiskow and Mawitnwyitchikan (Cris), Godfather: John Deschamps, Godmother: Therese Dagneau, P. Tissier priest o.m.i. (page 119)

Allary, Marguerite: See Louis Montagnais and Marguerite Allary

Amiskosit, Benjamin and Pauline Crise: M-7, Benjamin Amiskosit, married 18 April 1884, Pauline Crise, C. Scollen priest o.m.i. (page 98)

Amokiseyin, Alexandre: B-91, Alexandre Amokiseyin, baptized 14 October 1861, born yesterday, son of Amokiseyin and Josephte Crise, Godmother: Francoise Boucher, J. M. H. Caer priest o.m.i. (page 38)

Anderson, Elisa: B-8, Elisa Anderson, baptized 24 December 1865, born 1 December, natural daughter of Anderson and Jeanne Kionuesk, Godfather: Albert Courtepatte (signed), Godmother: Lucile Nakweyin, A. Andre priest o.m.i. (page 61)

Anderson, Elisa: See John Shields and Elisa Anderson

Anderson, Lucie: B-_, Lucie Anderson, baptized 5 December 1869, natural daughter of Marie Ducharme and Gaby Anderson, ch2ristened two months by [..] Andre, Godmother: Lucie Nakowin, H. LeDuc priest. (page 68)

Anderson, Sara: B-1, Sara Anderson, baptized 7 March 1875, born 17 December 1874, illegitimate child of John Gilbert Anderson and Marie Charron dit Ducharme, Godfather: Henri Paquette, Godmother: Isabelle Chalifoux, J. J. M. Lestanc priest o.m.i. (page 85)

Anihanis, Marie: B-39, Marie Anihanis, baptized 12 September 1858, age over one month, daughter of Anihanis and Kwotshis, Godmother: .. Roland, A. Lacombe priest o.m.i. (page 5)

Arcand, Betsey: B-148, Betsey Arcand, baptized 31 May 1863, age 7 months, daughter of Pierre Arcand and Magdeleine Ditawnew, Godfather: Joseph Gagnon, Godmother: Tastawitch, J. M. Caer priest o.m.i. (page 51)

Arcand, Magdeleine: B-134, Magdeleine Arcand, baptized 8 August 1863, age 2 months, daughter of Isidore Arcand and Louise Crise, Godfather: Joseph Gagnon, Godmother: Magdeleine Desnoyers, Alb. Lacombe priest o.m.i. (page 48)

Arcand, Marie: B-124, Marie Arcand, baptized 11 May 1863, age 2 months, daughter of Joseph Arcand and Josephte Crise, Godfather: Henri Paquet, Godmother: Cecile Durand, Alb. Lacombe priest o.m.i. (page 46)

Arnaud, Norbert: B-2, Norbert Arnaud, baptized 11 May 1874, age 5 months, of the legitimate marriage of Heleonard Arnaud and Elizabeth Chalifour, Godfather: Pierre Berard, Godmother: Louise his wife, J. Joseph Dupuis priest o.m.i. (page 83)

Arnaud, Pierre: B-6, Pierre Arnaud, baptized 23 May 1869, born January, of the legitimate marriage of Pierre Arnaud and Elisabeth Pierre Riche [?], Godfather: Joseph Paquet, Godmother: Cecile Dumont, V. Bourgine priest. (page 67)

Ashen, James Alexandre: B-19, James Alexandre Ashen, baptized 28 December 1884, age 14 days, son of John Ashen and Marie Fowley, Godfather: James Gibbons, Godmother: Nancy Irvine, H. Grandin priest o.m.i. (page 101)

Askiwawasis, Agathe: B-103, Agathe Askiwawasis, baptized 1 April 1862, age four months, daughter of Askewawasis and a Piche, Godfather: Michel Cardinal, Alb. Lacombe priest o.m.i. (page 41)

Askiwimustus, John: B-10, John Askiwimustus, baptized 10 January 1860, age 3 years, son of Ashiwimustus and a cousin of Alexis Piche, Godmother: Catherine Opetaskewok, Albert Lacombe priest o.m.i. (page 20-21)

Askiwimustus, Paul: B-11, Paul Askiwimustus, baptized 10 January 1860, age 2 years, son of Ashiwimustus and a cousin of Alexis Piche, Godmother: Catherine Opetaskewok, Albert Lacombe priest o.m.i. (page 21)

Assiniboine, Genevieve: B-65, Genevieve Assiniboine, baptized 3 March 1861, age 4 days, daughter of Jean-Baptiste Assiniboine and Ema, daughter of Grand Labiche, Godfather: Alexis Koutomahas, Alb. Lacombe priest o.m.i. (page 31-32)

Assiniboine, Moise: B-16, Moise Assiniboine, baptized 3 June 1883, age 2 weeks, son of Baptiste Assiniboine and Pauline, Godfather: Augustin Berard, Godmother: Elize Bruno, C. Scollen priest o.m.i. (page 91)

Assiniboine, Thomas: B-8, Thomas Assiniboine, baptized 14 October 1868, age 2 weeks, son of Xavier Assiniboine and Loiuse Mistikomin, Godmother: Catherine Hanihanis, Alb. Lacombe priest o.m.i. (page 65)

Astabet, Pierre: B-61, Pierre Astabet, baptized 1 March 1861, age about 80 years, Godfather: Alexis Okimawanis, Alb. Lacombe priest o.m.i. (page 31)

Atakkukup, Michel: B-132, Michel Atakkukup, baptized 8 August 1863, age one year, son of Atakkukup and Marie Crise, Godfather: Michel Kalliou, Godmother: Marianne Gaudry, Alb. Lacombe priest o.m.i. (page 48)

Ataskum, Susanne: B-85, Susanne Ataskum, baptized 23 July 1861, age one year, daughter of Ataskum and Susanne Komiwistikwan, Godfather: Gabriel Dumond, J. Caer o.m.i. (page 36)

Attikamek, Rosalie: B-101, Rosalie Attikamek, baptized 19 March 1862, age one month, daughter of Attikamek and Catherine Durand, Godfather: Alexis Cardinal, Alb. Lacombe priest o.m.i. (page 41)

Attaskwan, Louis: B-24, Louis Attaskwan, baptized 17 January 1860, age 3 months, son of Attaskwan and Konwastikwan, Godfather: Louis Batoche, Albert Lacombe priest o.m.i. (page 23)

Attaskwan, Thomas: B-45, Thomas Attaskwan, baptized 24 February 1861, age 2 years, son of Attaskwan and Onohakitshikamikwa, Godfather: Thomas Boucher, Alb. Lacombe priest o.m.i. (page 28)

Auger, Augustin: B-40, Augustin Auger, baptized 12 September 1858, age one month and a little, son of Augustin Auger and Rosalie Labonne, Godfather: Antoine Blondoin, Godmother: Marie Labonne Beaudoin, Albert Lacombe priest o.m.i. (page 5)

Auger, Augustin and Silvie Bruno: M-3, Augustin Auger, widower of Rosalie Beaudoin, married 18 March 1861, Silvie Bruno, minor daughter of Michel Bruno and Catherine Laderoute, Present: Michel Kalliou and Michel Bruno, Alb. Lacombe priest o.m.i. (page 33)

Ayamihayan, Pauline: B-159, Pauline Ayamihayan, baptized 5 April 1864, age about 15 days, daughter of Louis Ayamihayan and Susanne Ebwatis, Godfather: Baptiste Bruneau, Godmother: Susanne Bouchre, M. R. Remas priest o.m.i. (page 54)

Ayatowew, Marianne: B-10, Marianne Ayatowew, baptized 1 April 1883, age 6 months, daughter of Alexis Ayatowew and a Piegan - Iskwesis, Godmother: Marie Norris, C. Scollen priest o.m.i. (page 89)

Ayikusis, Elie: B-4, Elie Ayikusis, baptized 25 February 1872, age 8 days, son of Pierre Ayikusis and Catherine, his wife, Godfather: Henri Paquette, Godmother: Euphrosine Beauregard, J. Joseph Dupuis priest o.m.i. (page 77)

Aywashn/Awastin/Ayowastin

Awastin, Pierre: B-18, Pierre Awastin, baptized 3 February 1858, age one year, son of Awastin and Ketwekit, Godfather: Michel Ayutshon, Godmother: Marie Valais (Berland), A. Lacombe priest o.m.i. (page 3)

Aywashn, Pierre: B-24, Pierre Aywashn, baptized 31 January 1859, age 10 days, son of Pierre Aywashn and Ketwekit, Godfather: Noel Courtepatte, A. Lacombe priest o.m.i. (page 12)

Ayowastin, Pierre and Rosalie Mamakokwes: M-5, Pierre Ayowastin, married 14 February 1884, Rosalie Mamakokwes, C. Scollen priest o.m.i. (page 96)

Baillargeron, Marie: See Toussaint Labonne Beaudoin and Marie Baillargeron

St.Joachim, Fort Auguste (Fort Edmonton) 1858-1890

Barbeau, Ignace and Rosalie Goin: M-6, Ignace Barbeau, minor son of Antoine Barbeau and Marie Anne Goivin, married 28 October 1861, Rosalie Goin, minor daughter of Antoine Goin and Catherine Boucher, Present: Dosithe Sicard dit Carifel and Pierre St.Sauveur, P. Caer priest o.m.i. (page 38)

Barker, Madison and Christine Mathilda Myers: M-8, Madison Barker, married 21 April 1884, Christine Mathilda Myers, Witness: Lawrence Donovan (signed) and P. Garneau, C. Scollen priest o.m.i. (page 98)

Bateau, Flora: B-12, Flora Bateau (Kwenis), baptized 22 April 1866, age 3 months, of the legitimate marriage of Charles Bateau and Jayne Steveson, Godmother: Marie Rolland, A. Andre o.m.i. priest. (page 62)

Batoche, Isabelle: B-2, Isabelle Batoche, baptized 24 November 1871, age 2 months, of the marriage of Louis Batoche and Nisikapiman, his wife, Godmother: Isabelle Dick (Collin), A. Andre o.m.i. priest. (page 72)

Batoche, Marie: B-6, Marie Batoche, baptized 26 November 1871, age 6 years, of the marriage of Louis Batoche and Nisikapiman, Godfather: Charles Deschenaux, Godmother: Monique Dumet, V. Bourgine priest. (page 73)

Baudry, Andrew: B-6, Andrew Baudry, baptized 25 May 1873, born this morning, of Pierre Baudry and Jeanne Sakan, Godfather: Pierre ..., Godmother: Catherine his wife, J. Joseph Dupuis priest o.m.i. (page 81)

Beauchamp, Justine: B-28, Justine Beauchamp, baptized 8 May 1860, age 4 months and 2 days, legitimate daughter of Pierre Beauchamp and Nancy Ward, Godfather: Georges Hatson [Hudson], Godmother: Marie Rolland, C. M. Frain o.m.i. (page 24)

Beauchamp, Pierre and Nancy Ward: M-3, Pierre Beauchamp, adult son of Pierre Beauchamp and Marie Morin, married 21 December 1858, Nancy Ward, minor daughter of George Ward and Catherine, Witnesses: Antoine Galarneau and Alexandre Savard, A. Lacombe priest o.m.i. (page 8)

Beauchene, Isabelle: B-128, Isabelle Beauchene, baptized 4 March 1863, daughter of Joseph Beauchene and Josephte Flatt, Godfather: Samuel Cunningham, Godmother: Mary Jane Brazeau, Alb. Lacombe priest o.m.i. (page 47)

Beauchene, Joseph and Josephte Flatt [Flett]: M-2, Joseph Beauchene, married 3 October 1860, Josephte Flatt, minor daughter of James Flatt, Present: Olivier Seguin dit Laderoute and Pierre St.Sauveur, Alb. Lacome priest. o.m.i. (page 25)

Beauchene, Josephte: B-81, Josephte Beauchene, baptized 22 June 1861, age 10 days, daughter of Joseph Beauchene and Josephte Flatt, Godfather: Pierre Lebrun, Godmother: Marie Pied-noir, Alb. Lacombe priest o.m.i. (page 35)

Beaudoin, Jacques Labonne: B-12, Jacques Labonne (Beaudoin), baptized 3 February 1858, age one year, son of Pierre Labonne (Beaudoin) and Yakkwawiyepiw, Godfather: William Blandion, A. Lacombe priest o.m.i. (page 2)

Beaudoin, Toussaint Labonne and Marie Baillargeron: M-2, Toussaint Labonne Beaudoin, adult son of Baile Labonne Beaudoin, and Nannette Cardinal, married 28 February 1859, Marie Baillargeron, widow of Nayanislot [?], Witnesses: Johny Cunningham and Pierre Lebrun, M. R. Remas o.m.i. (page 12)

Beaudry, La Louise: See Alex Tourangeau and La Louise Beaudry

Beauregard, Charles and Marie Bellerose: M-12, Charles Beauregard, adult son of Charles Beauregard and Josette Kalliou, married 18 October 1864, Marie Bellerose, minor daughter of Olivier Bellerose and Josephte Savard, Present: Olivier Bellerose and Antoine Savard, Alb. Lacombe priest o.m.i. (page 56)

Beauregard, Euphrosine: Lee J. Baptiste L□hirondelle and Euphrosine Beauregard

Belanger, Monique: See Olivier Gowler and Monique Belanger

Bellerose, Anne Marie: B-36, Anne Marie Bellerose, baptized 25 September 1859, age about 3 months and 23 days, legitimate daughter of Olivier Bellerose and Josephte Savard, Godfather: Antoine Savard, Godmother: Helene Beauregard, C. M. Frain o.m.i. (page 15)

Bellerose, Benjamin: B-146, Benjamin Bellerose, baptized 9 June 1863, age 3 about months, son of Olivier Bellerose and Catherine Suprenant, Godfather: Abraham Salois, Godmother: Marie Sinclair, M. R. Remas priest o.m.i. (page 51)

Belrose, Helene: B-9, Helene Belrose, baptized 14 January 1866, born 8 January, of Olivier Belrose and Josette Savard, Godfather: Norbert Belrose, Godmother: Mary Rolland, A. Andre priest o.m.i. (page 61)

Bellerose, Josue: B-2, Josue Bellerose, baptized 7 October 1867, born 2 October, of the legtimate marriage of Benjamin Bellerose and __ Neault, Godfather and Godmother: Pascal Breland and his wife, H. LeDuc priest o.m.i. (page 63)

Bellerose, Marie: See Charles Beauregard and Marie Bellerose

Bellerose, Monique: B-17, Monique Bellerose, baptized 18 November 1866, born 16 November, of the legitimate marriage of Olivier Bellerose and Catherine Surprenant, Godfather: Norbert Bellerose, Godmother: Marguerite Savard, [...]. (page 63)

Bellerose, Olive: B-1, Olive Bellerose, baptized 6 January 1869, b. 4 January 1869, legitimate daughter of Olivier Bellerose and Catherine Surprenant, Godfather: Emilien Bellerose, Godmother: Marie Savard, V. Bourgine priest. (page 66)

Bellerose, Olive: See Louis Laurence and Olive Bellerose

Bellerose, Olive: See Joseph Benoit and Olive Bellerose

Benoit, Joseph and Olive Bellerose: M-2, Joseph Benoit, adult son of Louis Benoit and Marguerite Forcier, married 27 October 1868, Olive Bellerose, adult daughter of Olivier Bellerose and Josephte Savard, Present: Olivier Bellerose and Antoine Savard, Alb. Lacombe priest o.m.i. (page 65)

Berard, Marguerite: See Baptiste Deschamps and Marguerite Berard

(Berens), Jordy: B-5, Jordy (Berens), baptized 16 April 1887, age 14 days, son of Rosalie Berens and and unknown father, Godfather: Joseph Paul, Godmother: Nancy, H. Grandin o.m.i. (page 119)

Berland, Magdeleine: B-58, Magdeleine Berland, baptized 28 February 1861, age 11 months, daughter of Honore Berland and Angelique Dion, Godfather: Pierre Dion, Godmother: Marguerite Kaatshimyit, Alb. Lacombe priest o.m.i. (page 30)

Berland, Marie: B-41, Marie Berland, baptized 11 February 1861, age 20 days, daughter of Edouard Berland dit Valade and Genevieve Mondion, Godfather: Louis Gladu, Godmother: Genevieve Gray, J. M. St.Caer o.m.i. (page 27)

Bart (Bird), Betsy: B-21, Betsy Bart (Bird), baptized 2 [?] October 1886, age 15 days, daughter of James Bart and Marie Boucher, Godmother: .. Short, H. Grandin o.m.i. (page 116)

Bird, Henry Johny: B-12, Henry Johny Bird, baptized 29 September 1889, age 15 days, legitimate son of James Bird and Emilia Boucher, Godmother: Philomene Paquette, V. Vegreville o.m.i. (page 131)

Bird, Joe and Marie-Anne Paul: M-4, Joe Bird, son of the latge Thomas Bird and the late Isabelle, married 24 August 1886, Marie-Anne Paul, minor daughter of Johny Paul and Philomene Paquette, Witnesses: William Rowland Jr. (signed) and Joseph Paul, H. Grandin o.m.i. (page 113)

Bird, Johny: B-12, Johny Bird, baptized 14 August 1887, age 9 days, son of Joe Bird and Marie Anne Paul, Godmother: Catherine ..., Godfather: Johny Paul, H. Grandin, o.m.i. (page 120)

Bird, Thomas Oliver: B-7, Thomas Oliver Bird, baptized 13 May 1888, age 4 days, of the legitimate marriage of James Bird and Therese Boucher, Godmother: Sarah Bird, H. Grandin o.m.i. (page 124)

Bird, William: B-15, William Bird, baptized 3 November 1889, born yesterday, legitimate son of Job Bird and Marianne Paul, Godfather: Joseph Paul, Godmother: Philomene Paquette, V. Vegreville o.m.i. (page 132)

Bisson, Isabelle: B-21, Isabelle Bisson, baptized 15 January 1860, age 3 weeks, daughter of Jean Baptiste Bisson and Magdeleine L'Iroquois, Godfather: Antoine Blandion, jr., Godmother: Eloiza Blandoin, Albert Lacombe priest o.m.i. (page 23)

Bisson, Paul: B-50, Paul Bisson, baptized 20 September 1858, age one month, son of Jean Baptiste Bisson and Magdeleine Couret-Oreille, Godmother: Marie Amable Bruno, A. Lacombe priest o.m.i. (page 7)

Bisson, Therese: See Alexandre Savard and Therese Bisson

Blondin, Caroline: B-45, Caroline Blondoin, baptized 16 September 1858, baptized without condition, age 9 months, baptized by a protestant minister, legitimate daughter of Paul Blondoin and Esther Robillard, Godfather: Philippe Brillant, Godmother: Catherine Parent, C. M. Frain m.o.m.i. (page 6)

Blandion, Pierre: B-23, Pierre Blandion, baptized 5 February 1858, age 8 months, son of Pierre Blandion and Marguerite Katehimiyu, Godmother: ..., A. Lacombe priest o.m.i. (page 3)

Boucher, Marie: See Louis Gregoire and Marie Boucher

Boucher, Moise: B-19, Moise Boucher, baptized 15 January 1860, age one months, son of Jean Marie Boucher and Charlotte Omiosis, Godfather: Alexis Naud, Godmother: Marie Desjarlais, Albert Lacombe pre o.m.i. (page 22)

Boucher, Pierre and Marie Todd: M-4, Pierre Boucher, married 26 December 1870, Marie Todd, Present: Pierre Deschenaux and Antoine Goin, A. Andre priest o.m.i. (page 71)

Bourke, __: B-26, __ Bourke, baptized 9 November 1886, born today of __ Bourke and __ Laperante [?], Godfather: Francois P..., H. Grandin o.m.i. (page 117)

Bradshaw, Elizabeth: B-2, Elizabeth Bradshaw, baptized _ January 1888, age _, daughter of Annie Meaver, wife of Bradshaw, Godfather: Harry Meaver, Godmother: Eliza Shields, H. Grandin o.m.i. (page 123)

Bradshaw, Flora Jane: B-14, Flora Jane Bradshaw, baptized 14 October 1889, born 2 September 1889, of the legitimate marriage of __ Bradshaw and Anna Meaver, Godmother: Alice Harvin, V. Vegreville o.m.i. (page 131)

Brand, Abraham and Marie Anne Migouwasis: M-2, Abraham Brand, adult son of Joseph Brand and Marie, married Marie Anne Migouwasis, adult daughter of Migouwasis, Witnesses: Z. Lizee priest o.m.i. (signed) and Georges St.Cyr (signed), H. Grandin o.m.i. (page 111-112)

Brazeau, Antoine: B-34, Antoine Brazeau, baptized 25 July 1858, age 2 days, son of Antoine Brazeau and Josephte Mac, Godfather: Antoine Galarneau, Godmother: Angelique Lucier, A. Lacombe priest o.m.i. (page 5)

Brazeau, Charles Louis: B-42, Charles Louis Brazeau, baptized 12 September 1858, born 14 August, son of Edouard Brazeau and Marguerite Brabant, Godfather: John Cunningham (signed), Godmother: Rosalie L'Hyrondelle, A. Lacombe priest o.m.i. (page 6)

Brazeau, Charles Louis: S-1, Charles Louis Brazeau, buried 1 January 1860, age one year, 3 months, died 4 November, son of Edouard Brazeau and Marguerite Brabant, Witnesses: John Cunningham (signed) and Baptiste Courtepatte, C. M. Frain o.m.i. (page 19)

Brazeau, Charles Louis: B-145, Charles Louis Brazeau, baptized 17 April 1863, born yesterday, son of Edouard Brazeau and Marguerite Brabant, Godfather: John Cunningham (signed), Godmother: Rosalie L'Hyrondelle, Alb. Lacombe priest o.m.i. (page 51)

Brazeau, Charles Louis: S-10, Charles Louis Brazeau, buried 1 May 1863, age 13 days, Witnesses: Abraham Salois and Louis Kalliou, M. R. Remas priest o.m.i. (page 51)

Briand, Angelique: See Angus McDonald and Angelique Briand

Bruneau/Bruneault/Bruno

Bruno, Alexandre: B-52, Alexandre Bruno, baptized 11 October 1858, born today, legtimate son of Louis Bruno and Angele Dumond, Godfather: Alexys Dumond, Godmother: Marianne Bruno, C. M. Frain. (page 7)

Bruneau, Alexandre: B-1, Alexandre Bruneau, baptized 21 February 1888, born 19 February 1888, of the legitimate marriage of Alexis Bruneau and Agnes Deschamps, Godmother: Vitaline Espevatis, wife of Delorme, Blanchet priest o.m.i. (page 123)

Bruneault, Alexis and Agnes Deschamps: M-3, Alexis Bruneault, married 26 December 1870, Agnes Deschamps, Present: Pierre Deschenaux and Antoine Dion, A. Andre o.m.i. priest. (page 70)

Bruno, Celestine: B-39, Celestine Bruno, baptized 30 September 1859, born 3 September, of Alexys Bruno and Sophie, Godmother: Cecile Lemire, C. M. Frain o.m.i. (page 16)

St.Joachim, Fort Auguste (Fort Edmonton) 1858-1890

Bruno, Edouard: B-11, Edouard Bruno, baptized 2 February 1858, age 2 months, son of Pierre Bruno Piwabiskokapaw and Marie, Godfather: Edouard Berland, Godmother: Genevieve Mongnon, A. Lacombe priest o.m.i. (page 2)

Bruneau, Francois and Victoire Racette: M-5, Francois Bruneau, minor son of the deceased Baptiste Brunault, married 26 December 1870, Victoire Racette, minor daughter of Augustin Racette and Justine Gauoins, his wife, Present: Pierre Deschenaux and Roussel, A. Andre o.m.i. priest. (page 71)

Bruno, Genevieve: B-49, Genevieve Bruno, baptized 19 September 1858, age 2 days, daughter of Pierre Bruno and Marie Watjewisk, Godfather: Antoine Gouin, Godmother: Marguerite Opimuthewis, A. Lacombe priest. (page 7)

Bruneau, Isidore Piyesis: B-15, Isidore Piyesis (Bruneau), baptized 30 September 1866, born 10 September, of the legitimate marriage of Isidore Peyisis and Isabelle, Godmother: Lalouise, A. Andre o.m.i. priest. (page 62)

Bruno, Jean Baptiste: S-1, Jean Baptiste Bruno, buried 3 January 1859, age 70 years, Witnesses: Joseph Beaudry, Charles Gladu, and Augustin Auger, A. Lacombe priest o.m.i. (page 9)

Bruneault, Jean Baptiste: S-5, Jean Baptiste Bruneault, buried 2 October 1861, age 40 years, Witnesses: Jean Baptiste Courtepatte and William Monroe, J. M. Caer o.m.i. (page 37)

Bruno, Lisette: S-8 Lisette Bruno, buried 6 November 1862, age 45 years, Witnesses: Jean Baptiste Courtepatte and Thomas Kalliou, Alb. Lacombe priest o.m.i. (page 45)

Bruneau, Louis: B-13, Louis Bruneau, baptized 20 May 1866, born in the eve, of the legitimate marriage of Louis Bruneau and Angele Dumont, Godmother: Suzanne Dumont, A. Andre o.m.i. priest. (page 62)

Bruno, Marie: B-20, Marie Bruno, baptized 15 January 1860, age 3 days, daughter of Joseph Bruno and Isabelle Peyewemnop [?], Godfather: Jean Marie Boucher, Godmother: Louise Desjarlais, Albert Lacombe priest o.m.i. (page 22)

Bruneault, Marie: B-31, Marie Bruneault, baptized 26 July 1860, born 8 July, daughter of Jean Baptiste Bruneault and Marie Decoine, Godfather: James Ward, Godmother: Catherine Bruneault, M. R. Remas priest o.m.i. (page 24)

Bruneau, Nancy: B-7, Nancy Bruneau, baptized 11 July 1869, daughter of Joseph Bruneau and Catherine Ward, Godfather: Johny Toby [?], Godmother: Nancy, V. Bourgine priest. (page 68)

Bruno, Paul: B-87, Paul Bruno, baptized 25 July 1861, born today, son of Louis Bruno and Angele Dumont, Godfather: Jacques Dumont, Godmother: Rosalie Dumont, J. M. Caer. (page 36)

Brunet, Philias and Christine Cardinal: M-2, Philias Brunet, widower of Jane Foley married 25 October 1888, Christine Cardinal, minor daughter of the late Andre Cardinal and Rosalie Breland, Present: P. Bower (signed) and Mowalis (signed), H. Grandin o.m.i. (page 126)

Bruno, Silvie: See Augustin Auger and Silvie Bruno

Cairney, James Gaston: B-5, James Gaston Cairney, baptized 5 April 1890, born 13 December 1889, son of Thomas Patrick Cairney and Magory Anne Thone, Godfather: Mr. Degagne, Godmother: Mrs. Duplessis, L. Fouquet o.m.i. (page 135)

Cakutch, Johny: B-11, Johny Cakutch, baptized 26 December 1869, age one month, of the marriage of William Cakutch and __ Omamikkew, Godfather: Johny Folly [Foley], Godmother: Cecile Dumont, H. LeDuc priest. (page 68)

Calder, John Edwin: B-32, John Edwin Calder, baptized 2 December 1883, age 14 days, of John Calder and Jane Kenawatch, Godfather: Moise Page, Godmother: Elisa Fowley, H. Grandin priest o.m.i. (page 93)

Calder, Marie Marguerite: B-147, Marie Marguerite Calder, baptized 14 July 1863, age 2 months, daughter of William Calder and Marie Sinclair, Godfather: Abraham Salois, Alb. Lacombe priest o.m.i. (page 51)

Calder, Mary
B-17, Mary Calder, baptized 20 September 1885, age 4 days, daughter of Johny Calder and Julie [Jane Piche per C-14954], Godmother: Isabelle Mawtokwik, H. Grandin o.m.i. (page 107)

Calliou/Callioh

Calliou, Catherine: B-7, Catherine Calliou, baptized 23 December 1865, born 10 December, of the legitimate marriage of Thomas Calliou and Marie Finley, Godfather: Olivier Bellerose, Godmother: Catherine Surprenant, A. Andre priest o.m.i. (page 61)

Callioh, Peter: B-1, Peter Callioh, baptized 3 February 1885, born yesterday of the legitimate marriage of Louis Callioh and Annie MacDonald, Godfather: David Dagneau, Godmother: Marie Morin, H. Grandin o.m.i. (page 103)

Cameron, Caroline: B-119, Caroline Cameron, baptized 16 November 1862, age 3 days, daughter of Thomas Cameron and Susanne Mokkomitekkwe, Godfather: Louis Roussel, Godmother: Angelique Tessier, J. M. Caer o.m.i. (page 45)

Cameron, Eliza: See Henry Dick Collin and Eliza Cameron

Cameron, Marie: B-168, Marie Cameron, baptized 23 October 1864, born today,daughter of Thomas Cameron and Susanne Mokkomitekkwe [?], Godfather: Pierre St.Sauveur, Godmother: Marguerite Brazeau, M. R. Remas priest o.m.i. (page 56)

Cameron, Thomas: B-92, Thomas Cameron, baptized 10 November 1861, age 34 years, Godfather: Jean Baptiste Courtepatte, Godmother: Francoise Boucher, Alb. Lacombe priest o.m.i. (page 39)

Cameron, Thomas and Suanne Mokkomitekkwe: M-7, Thomas Cameron, married 11 November 1861, Susanne Mokkomitekkwe, Present: Joseph Beauchene and Dosithe Sicard dit Carifel, Alb. Lacombe priest o.m.i. (page 39)

Cameron, Thomas and Marie: M-5, Thomas Cameron, married 5 December 1869, Marie __, Present: Henry Paquette (signed) and Louis Paquette, H. Leduc priest. (page 68)

Capawis, Marie: B-6, Marie Capawis, baptized 22 October 1865, age 2 years, daughter of Jean Capawis and Catherine, Godfather: John Hudgson [the "g" is crossed out] (signed), A. Andre o.m.i. priest. (page 61)

Cardinal, Christine: See Philias Brunet and Christine Cardinal

Cardinal, Adam: B-13, Adam Cardinal, baptized 3 February 1858, age one year, son of Pierre Cardinal and Catherine Patakkns, Godmother: Genevieve Mondoin, A. Lacombe priest o.m.i. (page 2)

Cardinal, Alexis: B-4, Alexis Cardinal, baptized 8 January 1860, age one month, son of Jerome Cardinal and Bela Wesawikkumanapiw, Godmother: Marie Nipissing, Albert Lacombe priest o.m.i. (page 19)

Cardinal, Angelique: See Donal MacIvor and Angelique Cardinal

Cardinal, Caroline: B-10, Caroline Cardinal, baptized 6 July 1887, born yesterday, of Eleonore Cardinal [Desjarlais crossed out], and an unknown father, Godmother: Isabelle Laframboise, H. Grandin o.m.i. (page 120)

Cardinal, Catherine: B-22, Catherine Cardinal, baptized 30 January 1859, age 70 years, Godfather: Joseph Gray, A. Lacombe priest o.m.i. (page 11)

Cardinal, Daniel and Susanne Tchatcamokan: M-1, Daniel Cardinal, married 1 April 1883, Susanne Tchatcamokan, Witness: Father Niquet (signed Jos. Nugant), C. Scollen priest o.m.i. (page 89)

Cardinal, David: David Cardinal, March 1885 confirmation, H. Grandin o.m.i. (page 104)

Cardinal, Genevieve: B-23, Genevieve Cardinal, baptized 17 October 1886, born 15 October 1886, of the legitimate marriage of Daniel Cardinal and Suzanne Tchatchamngan, Godfather: Mons. A. A. Ringuette (signed), Z. Lizee priest o.m.i. (page 117)

Cardinal, Jacques: B-68, Jacques Cardinal, baptized 3 March 1861, age 5 months, son of Jacques Cardinal and Lisette daughter of Kamawiamustat, Godfather: Pierre Dion, Alb. Lacombe priest o.m.i. (page 32)

Cardinal, Joseph: B-102, Joseph Cardinal, baptized 20 March 1862, age over one year, son of Antoine Cardinal and Marie, Godfather: Louis Cardinal, Godmother: Susanne Courteoreille, Alb. Lacombe priest o.m.i. (page 41)

Cardinal, Lisette: B-8, Lisette Cardinal, baptized 10 January 1860, age 2 years, daughter of Jacques Cardinal and Samaskekabow, Godfather: Jean Baptiste Maskutebwan, Godmother: Euphrosine Carindal, Albert Lacombe priest. o.m.i. (page 20)

Cardinal, Magdeleine: B-118, Magdeleine Cardinal, baptized 11 May 1862, age 2 months, daughter of Edouard Cardinal and Marie Sikakweyon, Godfather: Lazare Hammelin, Godmother: Magdeleine Petit Briant, Alb. Lacombe priest o.m.i. (page 44)

Cardinal, Maggy Marie: B-5, Maggy Marie (Cardinal), baptized 16 April 1889, born .. April 1889, of Eleonore Cardinal and an unknown father, Godfather: John John, Godmother: Lizzie Meaver, C. M. Turcotte priest. (page 129)

Cardinal, Nancy: B-50, Nancy Cardinal, baptized 26 February 1861, age 10 months, daughter of Joseph Cardinal and Marianne Berland, Godmother: Angelique Berland, Alb. Lacome priest o.m.i. (page 29)

Cardinal, Philippe: B-3, Philippe Cardinal, baptized 8 January 1860, age one month, son of Joseph Cardinal and Niganamipekinam, Godfather: Louise Nepissing, Godmother: Magdeleine Malaterre, Albert Lacombe priest o.m.i. (page 19)

Castor, Jean Baptiste: S-7, Jean Baptiste of the Castor nation, buried 19 October 1862, age about 7 years, Witnesses: Antoine Savard and Alexandre Savard, Alb. Lacombe priest o.m.i. (page 44)

Cazeau, Louis Philipe and Mary Wragge: M-1, Louis Philipe Cazeau (signed Philipe Casault), legitimate adult son of Louis Godefroy Cazeau and Odile Hero, married 22 September 1887, Mary Wragge (signed Mary U... Wragge, legitimate adult daughter of Alfred ... Wragge and Mary Christine Munson, Witnesses: Janette Walker (signed), C. H. Tonnon [?] (signed), Frances M. Ross (signed), Antoine Prince [?] (signed), H. Grandin o.m.i. (page 121)

Charleau, Isabelle: B-2, Isabelle Charleau, baptized 11 February 1883, age 15 days, daughter of Charleau and Rosalie Kapiwastmat, Godmother: Marie Norris, C. Scollen priest o.m.i. (page 87)

St.Joachim, Fort Auguste (Fort Edmonton) 1858-1890

Citta, Augustin: B-14, Augustin Citta, baptized 3 February 1858, age 3 years, son of Citta and Apiniwokup, Godmother: Rosalie Labonne, A. Lacombe priest o.m.i. (page 2)

Citta, Catherine: B-16, Catherine Citta, baptized 3 February 1858, age 5 months, daughter of Citta and Apiniwokup, Godmother: Rosalie Labonne, A. Lacombe priest o.m.i. (page 3)

Claudi, Joseph: B-3, Joseph Claudi, baptized 17 March 1890, age over 2 months, son of Sale Claudi and Jane Thomas (x), of the District of Edmonton, Godmother: Annie Miver (x), Fouquet priest. (page 133)

Clover, Charles: B-10, Charles Clover, baptized 4 March 1866, age one month, of the legitimate marriage of Thomas Clover and Bethsey Paul, Godmother: Jeanne, A. Andre o.m.i. (page 61)

Collin, Henry Dick and Eliza Cameron: M-1, Henry Dick Collin, minor son of Richard Collin, married 28 June 1865, Eliza Cameron, minor daughter of Thomas Cameron, Present: Joseph Dick Collan and Thomas Cameron, Alb. Lacombe priest o.m.i. (page 59)

Collin, Marie: B-42, Marie Collin, baptized 30 September 1859, age nine days, daughter of Richard Collin and Nancy Courtepatte, Godmother: Marie Fouly; C. M. Frain o.m.i. (page 16)

Connors, Edward: Edward Connors, March 1885 confirmation, H. Grandin o.m.i. (page 104)

Courteoreille, Andre: B-46, Andre Courteoreille, baptized 17 November 1859, age one month, son of Charles Courteoreille and a Crise, Godmother: Jeanne Courteoreille, Albert Lacombe priest o.m.i. (page 17)

Courteoreille, Isabelle: See Charles Onigotesis and Isabelle Courteoreille

Courteoreille, Michel: B-5, Michel Courteoreille, baptized 21 January 1859, age 4 months, son of Michel Courteoreille and Kiwekat, Godfather: Michel Normand, A. Lacombe priest o.m.i. (page 10)

Courte-oreille, Michel: B-163, Michel Courte-oreille, baptized 4 September 1864, age about 40 years, Godfather: Richard Dick, Godmother: Genevieve Bruyere, M. R. Remas priest o.m.i. (page 55)

Courte-Oreille, Michel and Genevieve Kamikwakanel: M-11, Michel Courte-Oreille, married 4 September 1864, Genevieve Kamikwakanel, Present: Richer Dick (Collan) and Genevieve Bruyere, M. R. Remas priest. (page 55)

Courteoreille, Pierre: B-42, Pierre Courteoreille, baptized 11 February 1861, age 5 days, son of Joseph Courteoreille and Susanne Desjarlais, Godfather: Charles Johnston, Godmother: Silvie Bruno, J. M. St. Caer o.m.i. (page 27-28)

Courteoreille, Pierre: B-28, Pierre Courteoreille, baptized 1 October 1883, age 8 days, of the legitimate marriage of Antoine Courteoreille and Nancy, Godmother: wife of Blandion, H. Grandin priest o.m.i. (page 93)

Courteoreille, Sophie: B-104, Sophie Courteoreille, baptized 1 April 1862, age 5 months, daughter of Michel Courteoreille and Marie Crise, Godfather: Michel Cardinal, Alb. Lacombe priest o.m.i. (page 41)

Courtepatte, Joachim: B-80, Joachim Courtepatte, baptized 1 June 1861, born today, son of Jean Baptiste Courtepatte and Josephte Bellecourt, Godfather: Henri Colin, Godmother: Rosalie L'Hyrondelle, Alb. Lacombe priest o.m.i. (page 35)

Courte-Pate, Marguerite: B-161, Marguerite Courte-Pate, baptized 20 August 1864, born 4 days, daughter of Baptiste Courte-Pate and Amable Bellecourt [Josephte], Godfather: Samuel Cunningham (signed), Godmother: Jane Gladu, M. R. Remas priest o.m.i. (page 55)

Coutisse, Isabelle: B-7, Isabelle Coutisse, baptized 4 June 1873, age 3 months, daughter of Pierre Eiche Coutisse and Marie his wife of Lac des ..., Godfather: Francois Lemire, Godmother: Marie ..., J. Joseph Dupuis priest o.m.i. (page 81)
Cris/Crise

Crise, Angelique: B-126, Angelique Crise, baptized 12 May 1863, age over one year, daughter of Gabriel Cris and Josephte Crise, Godmother: Angelique Adam, Alb. Lacombe priest o.m.i. (page 46)

Crise, Elize: B-125, Elize Crise, baptized 11 May 1863, age 7 days, daughter of Pierre Cris and Elize Crise, Godfather: Alexandre Landry, Godmother: Marguerite Desjardins, Alb. Lacombe priest o.m.i. (page 46)

Crise, Isabelle: B-12, Isabelle Crise, baptized 27 December 1874, age 2 months, legitimate daughter of Marianne Crise and Charly Crise, Godfather: Henry Paquette, Godmother: Isabelle Chalifou, V. Vegreville priest. o.m.i. (page 85)

Cris, Patrice: B-7, Patrice Cris, baptized 18 March 1883, son of Thomas and Marie Cris, Godmother: Cecile, wife of Baptiste des Chams, C. Scollen priest o.m.i. (page 88)

Cris, Simon: B-7, Simon Cris, baptized 8 January 1860, age 2 weeks, son of Simon Cris and Isabelle Piche, Godfather: Jean Baptiste, Albert Lacombe priest o.m.i. (page 20)

Cunningham, Daniel: B-160, Daniel Cunningham, baptized 26 June 1864, born day before yesterday, son of John Cunningham and Rosalie L'Hyrondelle, Godfather: Wenceslas Bruneau, Godmother: Josephte Bellecourt, J. M. Caer o.m.i. (page 54)

Cunningham, Edouard: B-110, Edouard Cunningham, baptized 5 July 1862, born today, son of Johny Cunningham and Rosalie L'hyrondelle, Godmother: Marguerite Brazeau (signed), J. M. Caer o.m.i. (page 43)

Cunningham, Nancy: B-33, Nancy Cunningham, baptized 10 Jun 1858, age 13 days, daughter of Johny Cunningham and Rosaly L'Hyrondelle, Godfather: Jean Baptiste L'Hyrondelle, Godmother: Catherine Loyer, A. Lacombe priest o.m.i. (page 5)

Cunningham, Rachel: B-14, Rachel Cunningham, baptized 15 July 1866, born 4 July, of the legitimate marriage of John Cunningham and Rosalie L'hirondelle, Godfather: Olivier Belrose, Godmother: Olive Belrose, A. Andre o.m.i. priest. (page 62)

Dagneau, Adolphus: B-14, Adolphus Dagneau, baptized 14 September 1873, born 8 September, of the legitimate marriage of Isaac Dagneau and Julie Larence, Godfather: Daniel Dagneau, Godmother: Therese Dagneau, J. Joseph Dupuis priest o.m.i. (page 82)

Dagneau, Caroline: B-9, Caroline Dagneau, baptized 22 June 1884, age 6 weeks, of the legitimate marriage of Louis Dagneau and Sarah McDonald, Godfather: Donald Mac Ivor, Godmother: Angelique Cardinal, H. Grandin. (page 98)

Dagneau, Corbette and Sarah Donald: M-6, Corbette Dagneau, adult son of Isaac Dagneau and Julie Lawrence, married 20 September 1886, Sarah Donald, adult daughter of George Donald and Betsy Bryce, Present: Joe Donald and A. A. Ringuette (signed), H. Grandin o.m.i. (page 116)

Dagneau, Daniel and Betsy Cris: M-13, Daniel Dagneau, adult son of Isaac Dagneau and Julie Lawrence, married 29 December 1884, Betsy, adult daughter of Jimii chee Marie [?] Cris, Witnesses: Victor Pineau and Martin Divertissant, H. Grandin priest o.m.i. (page 101)

Dagneau, Elie: Elie Dagneau, March 1885 confirmation, H. Grandin o.m.i. (page 104)
90)

Dagneau, Elisabeth: B-10, Elisabeth Dagneau, baptized 29 June 1890, born 25 June 1890 at Edmonton, legitimate daughter of Corbet Dagneau and Sara nee Donnel, Godmother: Emerence Charlain, wife of Donald, (signed Emerance Charland), L. Fouquet priest. (page 138)

Dagneau, Elizabeth: B-1, Elizabeth Dagneau, baptized 13 January 1889, born 5 January 1889, of the legitimate marriage of David Dagneau and Marie Morin, Godfather: Elie Dagneau, Godmother: Therese Rabaska, H. Grandin o.m.i. (page 129)

Dagneau, Emerance: B-16, Emerance Dagneau, baptized 9 November 1884, age 21 days, daughter of David Dagneau and Marie Morin, Godfather: Louis Laframboise, Godmother: Julie Dagneau, H. Grandin priest o.m.i. (page 100)

Dagneau, Flora: B-14, Flora Dagneau, baptized 21 July 1888, born 19 July 1888, of the legitimate marriage of Corbett Dagneau and Sarah, Godmother: Marie Rose Dagneau, H. Grandin o.m.i. (page 125)

Dagneau, Francois: Francois Dagneau, March 1885 confirmation, H. Grandin o.m.i. (page 104)

Dagneault, Heli Isaac: B-5, Heli Isaac Dagneault, baptized 25 April 1869, born 20 April, son of the legitimate marriage of Isaac Dagneault and Julie Laurence, Godfather: Henri Paquette, Godmother: Cecile Dumont, V. Bourgine priest. (page 67)

Dagneau, Janvier: B-1, Janvier Dagneau, baptized 16 January 1887, born 1 January 1887, of the legitimate marriage of David Dagneau and Marie Morin, Godfather: Mathias, H. Grandin o.m.i. (page 119)

Dagneau, Louis Leon and Marie Lauere: M-1, Louis Leon Dagneau, legitimate adult son of Isaac Dagneau and Julie Larence, married 28 January 1884, Marie Lauere whose parents are unknown, Present: David Dagneau and Normand Vandale, H. Grandin priest o.m.i. (page 95)

Dagneau, Pierre: B-13, Pierre Dagneau, baptized 21 April 1883, age 4 days, son of David Dagneau and Marie Morrin, Godfather: Frank Picard, Godmother: Melanie, wife of Ad. McPherson, C. Scollen priest o.m.i. (page 90)

Degagne, Emma Georgella: B-6, Emma Georgella Degagne, baptized 3 May 1886, born 1 May, of the legitimate marriage of Alexis Degagne and Hortense Morencey, Godfather: Stanislas Ganes [?], Godmother: Domuella Georgina Roy, H. Grandin o.m.i. (page 111)

Degagne, Joseph Georges: B-3, Joseph Georges Degagne, baptized 3 March 1888, born yesterday of the legitimate marriage of Alexis Degagne (signed A. F. Degagne) and Hortense _ dit Morency, Godfather: Antoine Prince (signed), Godmother: Mathide Roy (signed), H. Grandin o.m.i. (page 123)

Degagne, Maria-Anna-Alexis: B-11, Maria-Anna-Alexis Degagne, baptized 24 September 1889, of the legitimate of Alexis Degagne and Octavie Gaucher dit Morency, Godfather: Joseph Picard, Godmother: Antoinette Roy, V. Vegreville o.m.i. (page 131)

Delorme, Adolphus Peter: B-3, Adolphus Peter Delorme, baptized 24 March 1889, age over one month, son of Alphonse Delorme and Maggy Chastellain, Godmother: Clara Norris, H. Grandin o.m.i. (page 129)

Delorme, Marguerite: B-18, Marguerite Delorme, baptized 8 September 1886, age 3 days, legitimate daughter of Edward Delorme and Vitaline Epwatis, Godmother: Nancy Hamelin, H. Grandin o.m.i. (page 115)

Delorme, Marguerite: B-20, Marguerite Delorme, baptized 25 September 1886, born 15 September 1886, of the legitimate marriage of Alphonse Delorme and Marguerite Sutherland, Godfather: Jean-Baptiste Surprenant, Godmother: Suzanne, wife Ayamihagan, J. J. M. Lestanc omi priest. (page 116)

Delorme, Marie Louise: B-10, Marie Louise Delorme, baptized 14 June 1888, born 8 June 1888, of the legitimate marriage of Edouard Delorme and Vitaline Epewatis, Godmother: Suzanne Ayawikayan, H. Grandin o.m.i. (page 125)

Deschamps, Agnes: See Alexis Bruneault and Agnes Deschamps

Deschamps, Alex: B-142, Alex Deschamps, baptized 15 February 1863, born yesterday, son of Francois Deschamps and Marguerite Canada, Godfather: Michel Gray, J. M. Caer o.m.i. (page 50)

Deschamps, Alexandre: B-12, Alexandre Deschamps, baptized 24 June 1888, age 8 days, of the marriage of Joseph Deschamps and Therese Dagneau, Godfather: Louis Dagneau, Godmother: Marie Morin, H. Grandin o.m.i. (married Flora L'Hairondelle [L☐Hirondelle], 19 May 1913. (page 125)

Deschamps, Baptiste and Marguerite Berard: M-2, Baptiste Deschamps, minor son of Francois Deschamps and the deceased Marguerite Canada, married 17 April 1871, Marguerite Berard, minor daughter of Eustache Berard and Marguerite Primault, Present: Henri Paquette and Eustache Berard, A. Andre o.m.i. priest. (page 75)

Deschamps, Baptiste: B-5, Baptiste Deschamps, baptized 4 May 1872, born 3 May, of the legitimate marriage of Baptiste Deschamps and Marguerite Berard, Godfather: David Dagneault, Blanchet priest o.m.i. (page 77)

Deschamps, Henri: B-5, Henri Deschamps, baptized 27 April 1872, legitimate son of Francois Deschamps and Virginie Berland, Godfather: Edouard Boucher, Godmother: Emilia Calder, belle fille William Munroe, J. Joseph Dupuis priest. o.m.i. (page 78)

Deschamps, Johny Rabaska: B-8, Johny Deschamps dit Rabaska, baptized 29 June 1889, age 4 days, legitimate son of Jean-Baptiste Deschamps dit Rabasca and Marguerite Berard, Godfather: Antoine Dion, Godmother: Marie Rose Belanger, V. Vegreville o.m.i. (page 130)

Deschamps, Justine Rabaska: B-8, Justine Rabaska or Deschamps, baptized 1 June 1890, born 29 May 1890, daughter of Joe Deschamps or Rabaska and Therese (nee Dagnon), Godfather: Eli Dagnon, Godmother: Marie Rose, L. Fouquet priest. (page 137)

Deschamps, Marguerite: See Daniel Paul and Marguerite Deschamps

Deschamps, Paul: B-89, Paul Deschamps, baptized 27 September 1861, born yesterday, son of Francois Deschamps and Marguerite Hainault, Godmother: Marie Sapin dit Campion, J. M. Caer o.m.i. (page 37)

Deschenaux, Domitilde: B-6, Domitilde Deschenaux, baptized 8 December 1870, born yesterday, of the legitimate marriage of Pierre Deschenaux and Josephine Courchene, his wife, Godfather: Joseph Deschenaux, son, Godmother: Angelique, his wife, V. Bourgine priest. (page 70)

Desjarlais, Etienne and Joseph: B-76 and B-77, Etienne and Joseph Desjarlais, twins, baptized 10 May 1861, age 2 days, sons of Paul Desjarlais and Lisette Bruneault, Godfather: Joseph Courteoreille, Godmother: Susanne Desjarlais, M. R. Remas p.o.m.i. (page 34)

Deslauriers, Marie Anne (Denoyer): B-46, Marie Anne Deslauriers (Denoyer), baptized 16 September 1858, baptized without condition age 10 months, baptized by a protestant minister, legitimate daughter of Louis Deslauriers (Denoyer) and Marie Anne Baudry, Godfather: Philippe Brillant, Godmother: Catherine Parent, C. M. Frain m.o.m.i. (page 6)

Dion, Augustin: B-57, Augustin Dion, baptized 28 February 1861, age 10 months, son of Pierre Dion and Marguerite Ka at ehi wey it, Godfather: Alexis Cardinal, Alb. Lacombe priest o.m.i. (page 30)

Dion, Nancy: B-88, Nancy Dion, baptized 26 September 1861, age 12 days, daughter of Antoine Dion and Marie Desjarlais, Godfather: Pierre Lebrun, Godmother: Marie Pied-Noir, J. M. Caer o.m.i. (page 37)

Donald, Mary Louise: B-15, Mary Louise Donald, baptized 22 August 1886, age one month, daughter of Sara Donald, Godmother: Rosalie Berard, Z. Lizee priest o.m.i. (page 113)

Donald, Peter and Isabelle Paquette: M-4, Peter Donald, protestant, adult son of George Donald and Bethsy Brass, born at Stone Fort, Manitoba and living at Edmonton, Alberta, widower of Louisa (Crise) his first wife, married 11 April 1890, Isabelle Paquette, catholic, minor daughter of Louis Paquette and Julie Dagneau, born and living at Edmonton, Present: Joe Donald (x) and Thomas Ward (x), V. Vegreville o.m.i. (page 135-136)

Donald, Sarah: See Corbette Dagneau and Sarah Donald

Ducharme, Joseph: B-18, Joseph Ducharme, baptized 25 November 1866, born 21 November, son of Marie Ducharme, Godfather: Joseph Beauchene, A. Andre priest o.m.i. (page 63)

Dumay, Helene: B-8, Helene Dumay, baptized 9 August 1874, age 18 days, legitimate daughter of Charles Dumay and Marie St.Arnaud, Godfather: Frederic durocher, Godmother: Helene Bauregard, J. Joseph Dupuis priest. o.m.i. (page 84)

Dumet, Marguerite and Adelaide: B-53 and B-54, Marguerite and Adelaide Dumet, baptized 13

St.Joachim, Fort Auguste (Fort Edmonton) 1858-1890

December 1858, age 16 days, daughters of Charles Dumet and Marie St.Arnaud, Godfather: John Cunningham (signed) and Louis Bouvet, Godmother: Catherine Gladu and Angelique Lucier, A. Lacombe priest o.m.i. (page 7)

Dumond, Marie: B-38, Marie Dumond, baptized 18 September 1859, born today, of Francois Dumond and Nancy Gladu, Godfather: Antoine Savard, Godmother: Marguerite Bisson, C. M. Frain m.o.m.i. (page 15)

Dumont, Alfred: B-4, Alfred Dumont, baptized 18 July 1870, born 3 July, of the legitimate marriage of Isidore Dumont and Judith Parenteau, Godfather: Raphael [Parenteau], V. Tourmond priest. (page 69)

Dumont, Jean Baptiste and Philomene Vanasse: M-2, Jean Baptiste Dumont, son of the deceased Gabriel (Napokes), married 22 April 1872, Philomene Vanasse, daughter of J. B. Vanasse and Catherine Cardinal, Witnesses: Joseph Allard, the father J. B. Hanasse, William Munro, and Francois Deschamp, J. Joseph Dupuis priest o.m.i. (page 77)

Dumont, Veronique: See William Hamilton and Veronique Dumont

Duplessis, Louis Joseph Alphonse: B-11, Louis Joseph Alphonse Duplessis, baptized 29 June 1890, born 2 June 1890, legitimate child of Raphael Duplessis (signed) and Elise nee Morency, Godfather: Joseph Kelly (signed), Godmother: Euelina Duplessis, L. Fouquet o.m.i. (page 138)

Duplessis, Thomas: B-2, Thomas Duplessis, baptized 7 March 1889, born today, of the legitimate marriage of Raphael Duplessis and Elisa Morence, Godfather: A. Degagne, H. Grandin o.m.i. (page 129)

Duquet, Antoine: B-43, Antoine Duquet, baptized 16 September 1858, age 9 months, natural son of Genevieve Duquet, Godfather: Philippe Brillant, Godmother: Catherine Parent, C. M. Frain m.o.m.i. (page 6)

Duquet, Genevieve: B-131, Genevieve Duquet, baptized 8 August 1863, age one month, daughter of Joseph Duquet and Marianne, Godmother: Genevieve Savoyard, Alb. Lacombe priest o.m.i. (page 48)

Duquet, Genevieve: See Frank Johnson and Genevieve Duquet

Duquette, Nancy: B-4, Nancy Duquette, baptized 10 May 1873, daughter of William Duquette and Jeanne daughter of Iskwanak, his wife,, Godfather: Alexander Piyesimul, Godmother: Marie Anihanis, J. Joseph Dupuis priest o.m.i. (page 80)

Duquette, William and Jeanne Kamikwanwanaw: M-3, William Duquette, son of Joseph Duquette, married 12 May 1872, Jeanne Kamikwanwanaw, daughter of Iskwanok Kamikwanwanaw, Witnesses: Pierre Lebrun, Iskwanok Kamikwanwanaw, J. B. Napesew, Francois Deschamp, and Henri Paquette, J. Joseph Dupuis priest. (page 78)

Durand, Catherine: B-54, Catherine Durand, baptized 27 February 1861, age 2 years, daughter of Paul Durand and Kotakupet, Godfather: Francois Deschamp, Godmother: Marguerite Hainault, Albert Lacombe priest o.m.i. (page 29)

Durand, Catherine: B-56, Catherine Durand, baptized 28 February 1861, age 2 years, daughter of Louis Durand and Okatshiken, Godfather: Francois Deschamps, Godmother: Catherine Pakak, Alb. Lacombe priest o.m.i. (page 30)

Durand, Sophie: B-53, Sophie Durand, baptized 27 February 1861, age 4 years, daughter of Paul Durand and Kotakupet, Godfather: Alexis Okimawasis, Albert Lacombe priest o.m.i. (page 29)

Durand, Susanne: B-55, Susanne Durand, baptized 28 February 1861, age 4 years, daughter of Louis Durand and Okatshiken, Godfather: Pierre Cardinal, Alb. Lacombe priest o.m.i. (page 30)

Ebwatit/Ebuatit:

Ebwatit, Joseph: B-72, Joseph Ebwatit, baptized 8 March 1861, age 2 days, son of Joseph Ebwatit and Catherine Bruneault, Godfather: Antoine Auger, Godmother: Louise Boucher, J. M. St. Caer priest o.m.i. (page 33)

Ebwatit, Joseph: B-2, Joseph Ebwatit, baptized 29 March 1868, age 2 months, son of Joseph Ebwatit and Catherine Bruneault, Godmother: Philomene Paquet, Alb. Lacombe priest o.m.i. (page 64)

Ebuatit, Nancy: B-143, Nancy Ebuatit, baptized 26 March 1863, age one month, daughter of Joseph Ebuatit and Catherine Bruneault, Godmother: Rosalie L'Hyrondelle, J. M. Caer o.m.i (page 50)

Etawatchabew, Magdeleine: B-44, Magdeleine Etawatchabew, baptized 1 October 1859, age 6 days, daughter of Etawatchabew and Cecile Crise, Godfather: George Hatson, Godmother: Louise Laderoute, Albert Lacombe priest o.m.i. (page 17)

Etewakkew, Angelique: B-66, Angelique Etewakkew, baptized 3 March 1861, age 6 years, daughter of Joseph Etewakkew and Wabikkewe, Godfather: Alexis Okimawasis, Alb. Lacombe priest o.m.i. (page 32)

Eyabet, Francois: B-106, Francois Eyabet, baptized 1 April 1862, age one month, son of Eyabet and Susanne Apistiskwesis, Godfather: Michel Cardinal, Alb. Lacombe priest o.m.i. (page 42)

Eyabet, Susanne: B-107, Susanne Eyabet, baptized 1 April 1862, age 4 years, daughter of Eyabet and Susanne Apistiskwesis, Godfather: Michel Cardinal, Alb. Lacombe priest o.m.i. (page 42)

Fabre, Adam: B-7, Adam Fabre, baptized 20 June 1874, age 5 days, legitimate son of Paul Fabre and Monique Dumay, Godfather: Daniel Dagnault, Godmother: Marguerite Berard, wife of Deschamps, J. Joseph Dupuis priest. o.m.i. (page 84)

Favel, Louis: B-1, Louis Favel, baptized 7 March 1868, born 29 February, of the legitimate marriage of Louison Favel and Judith Misotesis, Godfather: Norbert Bellerose, H. Leduc priest o.m.i. (page 64)

Flett, Andrew and Marie Paul: M-1, Andrew Flett, legitimate minor son of William Flett and __ Cameron, married 4 May 1868, Marie Paul, legitimate minor daughter of Paulette Paul and Josephte Crise, Witnesses: Noel Courteoreille and Benjamin Vandale, H. Leduc priest o.m.i. (page 64)

Flett, Johny: B-8, Johny Flett, baptized 20 July 1869, born 10 days, of the legitimate marriage of Andrew Flett and Marie Paul, Godfather: Octave Bellerose, Godmother: Philomene Paul, H. Leduc priest. (page 68)

Flatt [Flett], Josephte: See Joseph Beauchene and Josephte Flatt [Flett]

Foley/Folly/Folay

Folly, Jeanne: B-75, Jeanne Folly [Foley], baptized 8 April 1861, age 5 days, daughter of James Folly and Jeanne, Godfather: James Ward, Godmother: Catherine Bruneau, J. M. St. Caier priest o.m.i. (page 34)

Foley, Jeanne: S-3, Jeanne Foley, buried 4 May 1861, age one month, daughter of James Foley and Jeanne, Witnesses: Jean Baptiste Courtepatte and Josephte Bellecourt, J. M. St.Caier priest o.m.i. (page 34)

Folay, Marie: B-29, Marie Folay [Foley], baptized 9 May 1858, age 4 months, daughter of John Folay and Eugenie Nankisik, Godfather: Joseph Allard, Godmother: Marie Contois, M. R. Remas p.o.m.i. (page 4)

Fosseneuve, Nancy: B-7, Nancy Fosseneuve, baptized 26 December 1870, born yesterday, of the legitimate marriage of Jean Baptiste Bougillier (Fosseneuve) and Marie Desjarlais, Godfather: Pierre Gabriel (Dumont), Godmother: Rosalie Gabriel [Dumont], A. Andre o.m.i. priest. (page 70)

Gadoua, Marguerite: B-12, Marguerite Gadoua, baptized 15 September 1872, age 2 days, daughter of the legitimate marriage of ... Gadoua and Suzanne, Cree woman, Godfather: Jospeh Macaron, Godmother: Marguerite Berard, ... Andre Blanchy priest o.m.i. (page 79)

Garneau, Henri Joseph: B-4, Henri Joseph Garneau, baptized 22 March 1890, born 20 March 1890, of Laurent Garneau and Eleonore, Godfather: Baptiste Deschamps, Godmother: Marguerite McDonald, L. Fouquet priest. (page 134)

Garneau, Jean-Marie: B-2, Jean-Marie Garneau, baptized 10 January 1886, age 12 days, son of Laurent Garneau and Eleonore Thomas, Godfather: A. F. Degagne (signed), Godmother: G. M.. Holly (signed), H. Grandin o.m.i. (married 28 November 1908 Anne Goulet at Strathcona) (page 110)

Garneau, Louis: Louis Garneau, March 1885 confirmation, H. Grandin o.m.i. (page 104)

Garneau, Maliny: B-13, Maliny Garneau, baptized 15 July 1888, born 9 July 1888, of the legitimate marriage of Lawrence Garneau and Eleonore Thomas, Godfather: Louis Laframboise, Godmother: Isabelle, his wife, H. Grandin o.m.i. (page 125)

Gaucher, Genevieve: B-156, Genevieve Gaucher, baptized 25 February 1864, age about one month, daughter of Joseph Gaucher and Eloiza Dion, Godfather: Henri Collin, Godmother: Marie Desjarlais, M. R. Remas priest o.m.i. (page 53)

Gaucher, Patrick: B-99, Patrick Gaucher, baptized 17 March 1862, age one month, son of Joseph Gaucher and Eloiza Dion, Godfather: Alexis Cardinal, Godmother: Colette Gaucher, Alb. Lacombe priest o.m.i. (page 41)

Gauvreau, Georges Lewis: B-25, Georges Lewis Gauvreau, baptized 9 November 1886, born yesterday, of the legitimate marriage of Pierre Valmore Gauvreau and Harriet Mary Laurin, Godfather: Georges Roy, Godmother: f. Roy, H. Grandin o.m.i. (page 117)

Gauvreau, Louis: B-9, Louis Gauvreau, baptized 3 May 1885, born 3 May, of the legitimate marriage of P. V. Gauvreau (signed) and Harriet Mary Laurin, Godfather: Luke Kelly (signed), Godmother: Elizabeth Kelly (signed), H. Grandin priest o.m.i. (page 105)

Gauvreau, Marie Celine: B-10, Marie Celine Gauvreau, baptized 4 August 1889, born 2 August 1889, of the legitimate marriage of Pierre Louis Francois Valmore Gauvreau and Henriette Marie Laurie, Godfather: Raphael Duplessis (signed), Godmother: Elise Morency (signed), L. Fouquet o.m.i., H. Grandin o.m.i. (page 130)

Gauvreau, Marie Corine: B-13, Marie Corine Gauvreau, baptized 18 August 1890, born 16 August 1890 at Edmonton, daughter of Pierre Valmore Gauvreau (signed) and Harriette Marie (nee Laurie), Godfather: Mr. Stanislas Larue (signed), Godmother: Lecia Saint Jean (signed), L. Fouquet omi. (page 138)

St.Joachim, Fort Auguste (Fort Edmonton) 1858-1890

Gauvreau, Pierre Michael Ubald: B-4, Pierre Michael Ubald Gauvreau, baptized 6 March 1888, born yesterday, of the legitimate marriage of Pierre Valmore Gauvreau and Harriet Mary Laurie, Godfather: Ubold Prince (signed), Godmother: Georgiana Foisy (signed Dame J. Kelly), H. Grandin o.m.i. (page 123)

Genereux, Edouard: B-115, Edouard Genereux, baptized 11 May 1862, age 20 days, son of Edouard Genereux and Marie Chatelain, Godmother: Marianne Gaudry, Alb. Lacombe priest o.m.i. (page 44)

Gibbons, Louise: B-7, Louise Gibbons, baptized 27 May 1889, born 19 April 1889, of James Gibbons and Mary Isabelle Gouin, Godmother: Marie, wife of Jacques Norris, A. Lacombe priest omi. (married John O'Sullivan 28 May 1913) (page 130)

Gibbons, Rose Mary: B-8, Rose Mary Gibbons, baptized 15 May 1887, age 2 months, daughter of James Gibbons and Mary Isabelle Gouin, Godfather: Patrick Byrns (signed) , Godmother: Catherine wife of Byrns, H. Grandin, o.m.i. (page 120)

Gibbons, William Edward: B-18, William Edward Gibbons, baptized 10 June 1883, age 6 weeks, son of James Gibbons and Mary Gouin, Godfather: James Norris, Godmother: Lucie Sanderson, C. Scollen priest o.m.i. (page 91)

Gladstone, Helene: B-86, Helene Gladstone, baptized 4 July 1861, born today, daughter of William Gladstone and Henriette Le Blanc, Godmother: Jane Souliers, J. M. St. Caer o.m.i. (page 36)

Gladstone, Henriette: B-31, Henriette Gladstone, baptized 9 May 1859, age 2 months, legitimate daughter of William Gladstone and Henriette Leblanc, Godfather: Louis Bouvet, Godmother: Angelique Maskegone [?], C. M. Frain m.o.m.i. (page 13)

Gladu (See Also Quinn)

Gladu, Albert: B-26, Albert Gladu, baptized 10 September 1883, age 3 weeks, son of Johnny Gladu and Julie Crise, Godmother: Eliza Gladu, H. J. H. Blais priest o.m.i. (page 92)

Gladu, Alexandre: B-14, Alexandre Gladu, baptized 15 April 1871, age 2 months, of George Gladu and Anny Kistinahowe, Godfather: Charles Gladu, Godmother: Marie St.Arnaud, A. Andre o.m.i. priest. (page 74)

Gladu, Caroline: B-6, Caroline Gladu, baptized 24 February 1883, age one month, daughter of Johnny Gladu and Marguerite [Crise crossed out and Bruno written in a different hand], Godfather: Father Lavoie o.m.i. (signed Jeremie Lavoie), C. Scollen priest o.m.i. (page 88)

Gladu, Charles: B-10, Charles Gladu, baptized 1 September 1872, age 9 months, son of Charles Gladu and Jeanny [House crossed out] Gray, his wife, Godmother: Madeleine Campeau, J. Joseph Dupuis priest o.m.i. (page 79)

Gladu, Edouard and Adelaide: B-12 & 13, Edouard Gladu, age one year, and Adelaide Gladu, age 3 months, baptized 31 August 1873, legitimate children of Edouard Sates Gladu and Sophie his wife, Godfather: Augustin Berard and Marguerite his wife, J. Joseph Dupuis priest o.m.i. (page 82)

Gladu, Edouard Sates: M-4, Edouard Sates Gladu, married 31 August 1873, Sophie Iyakwekitawas, Witnesses: Augustin Berard and Bernard l'Iroquois, J. Joseph Dupuis priest o.m.i. (page 82)

Gladu, Emilie Madeline: B-1, Emilie Madeline Gladu, baptized 31 December 1882, age 6 days, of the legitimate marriage of Celestin Gladu and Marguerite Calliho, Godfather: Johnny Paul, Godmother: Annie Gladu, C. Scollen priest o.m.i. (page 86)

Gladu, Francois: B-11, Francois Gladu, baptized 20 September 1874, infant of Georges Gladu and Ann ...., Godfather: Abraham Cardinal, Godmother: Genevieve Duquette, ... priest o.m.i. (page 85)

Gladu, George and Marie Kitchwatnim [?]: M-2, George Gladu, married 24 January 1884, Marie Kitchwatnim [?], Witnesses: Charles Gladu and Jane, C. Scollen priest o.m.i. (page 95)

Gladu, George: B-28, George Gladu, baptized 19 December 1886, age one month, son of George Quinn and Annie, Godfather: Charles Quinn, H. Grandin o.m.i. (page 118)

Gladu, Isabelle: See Joe Quinn alias Gladu and Isabelle Gladu

Gladu, Jammy and Anne Mominawatow: M-5, Jammy Gladu, legitimate adult son of Joseph Gladu dit Eskinikiw and Emma Bellecourt, married 30 September 1885, Anne Mominawatow, minor daughter of Mominawatow and Anne .. Grant, Present: R. P. Meaver (signed) and P. Blodeau [?], H. Grandin o.m.i. (page 107)

Gladu, Johnny: B-1, Johnny Gladu, baptized 14 January 1883, age 2 weeks, son of Alice Gladu, Godfather: Eleuaire Arnaux, Godmother: Olive Shalifou, C. Scollen priest o.m.i. (page 87)

Gladu, Johnny: B-8, Johnny Gladu, baptized 18 March 1883, age 2 weeks, son of Charles Gladu and Jane, Godmother: Eliza Gladu, C. Scollen priest o.m.i. (page 88)

Gladu, Joseph: B-11, Joseph Gladu, baptized 1 September 1872, age 8 months, son of Johnny Gladu and Julie, his wife, Godmother: Marguerite wife of Cameron, J. Joseph Dupuis priest o.m.i. (page 79)

Gladu, Patrice: B-22, Patrice Gladu, baptized 5 August 1883, age 2 weeks, son of William Gladu and Emma Crise, Godfather: Baptiste Cris, Godmother: __ Dumais, H. J. H. Blais priest o.m.i. (page 92)

Gladu, Sarah: B-19, Sarah Gladu, baptized 10 June 1883, age 5 weeks, daughter of Alexandre Gladu and Marianne Nabesis, Godfather: Joseph Paul, Godmother: Elize Maver, C. Scollen priest o.m.i. (page 91)

Gladu, Therese: B-62, Therese Gladu, baptized 2 March 1861, age 4 years, daughter of Nabes Gladu and Marguerite Wabistikwan, Godfather: Pierre Beaudoin, Alb. Lacombe priest o.m.i. (page 31)

Gladu, Therese: B-155, Therese Gladu, baptized 22 February 1864, age about one month, daughter of Rosalie Gladu, Godfather: John Hudson, Godmother: Betsey Paul, M. R. Remas priest o.m.i. (page 53)

Gladu, Thomas: B-63, Thomas Gladu, baptized 2 March 1861, age one year, son of Nabes Gladu and Marguerite Wabistikwan, Godfather: Pierre Beaudoin, Alb. Lacombe priest o.m.i. (page 31)

Gladu, Timmy Bateau: B-6, Timmy Gladu dit Bateau, baptized 6 May 1888, age 3 months, son of Charles Gladu dit Bateau and Jane Thomas, Godfather: Alec _, Godmother: Annie Bradshaw, H. Grandin o.m.i. (page 124)

Gladu, Veronique: Georges Ward and Veronique Gladu

Gladu, William: B-41, William Gladu, baptized 12 September 1858, age 5 days, son of Paul Gladu and Marie Labonne Beaudoin, Godfather: William Beaudoin, Godmother: Rosalie Labonne Beaudoin, A. Lacombe priest o.m.i. (page 6)

Gladu, William: S-2, William Gladu, buried 20 August 1860, age over one year, son of Paul Gladu and Marie Beaudoin, Witnesses: William Dion and George Hudson, Alb. Lacombe priest o.m.i. (page 24-25)

Godin, Antoine: B-41, Antoine Godin, baptized 30 September 1859, age 2 months, son of Antoine Godin and Susanne Bruno, Godfather: James Richard, Godmother: Judith Godin, C. M. Frain o.m.i. (page 16)

Godin, Constantin: B-2, Constantin Godin, baptized 23 April 1865, age 9 days, son of Antoine Godin and Susanne Bruneault, Godmother: Louise Brueanult, Alb. Lacombe priest o.m.i. (page 59)

Godin, Georges and Louisa: M-9, Georges Godin, son of the late Antoine Godin and Suzanne Bruneau, married 27 November 1885, Louisa, widow of Pierre Nabises Ma..., Present: R. P. Leduc and J. Bilodeau, H. Grandin o.m.i. (page 109)

Godin, Suzanne: B-18, Suzanne Godin, baptized 12 December 1884, age 3 weeks, daughter of .. Godin and Marie Crise, Godmother: Josephte Crise, H. Grandin priest o.m.i. (page 101)

Godin, William: S-6, William Godin, buried 15 March 1862, age 5 months, son of Antoine Godin and Susanne Bruneault, Witnesses: Louis Roussel and Antoine Savard, Alb. Lacombe priest o.m.i. (page 40)

Goin/Gouin

Goin, Isabelle: B-98, Isabelle Goin, baptized 30 March 1862, born 26 March, daughter of Antoine Goin and Francoise Boucher, Godfather: Ignace Barbeau, Godmother: Rosalie Goin, J. M. Caer o.m.i. (page 40)

Gouin, Marie Louise: B-12, Marie Louise Gouin, baptized 27 May 1885, age 7 days, legitimate daughter of Augustin Gouin and Emelie Munro, Godfather: Francois Deschamps dit Rabaska, Godmother: Julie Munro, H. Grandin o.m.i. (page 106)

Gouin, Mary Isabelle: Mary Isabelle [Gouin] wife of Gibbons, March 1885 confirmation, H. Grandin o.m.i. (page 104)

Goin, Rosalie: See Ignace Barbeau and Rosalie Goin

Gowler, Olivier and Monique Belanger: M-1, Oliver Gowler (signed), married 28 April 1886, Monique Belanger, minor daughter of the late __ Belanger and Julie ..., Witnesses: George Norris (signed) and James Gibbons (signed), H. Grandin o.m.i. (page 110-111)

Gregoire, Louis and Marie Boucher: M-4, Louis Gregoire, adult son of the deceased Jean Baptiste Gregoire and Isabelle St.Pierre, married 1 October 1861, Marie Boucher, adult daughter of the deceased Joseph Boucher and the deceased Marguerite Dupuis, Present: Antoine Gouin and Bazile Hebert, Alb. Lacombe priest o.m.i. (page 37)

Hamelin/Hammelin:

Hammelin, Abraham: B-22, Abraham Hammelin, baptized 16 January 1860, age 5 days, son of Antoine Hammelin and Isabelle Bruno, Godfather: Louis Batoche, Albert Lacombe priest o.m.i. (page 23)

Hammelin, Albert: B-151, Albert Hammelin, baptized 19 September 1863, age 15 days, son of Antoine Hammelin and Susane Bruneault, Godmother: Rosalie Bruneault, Alb. Lacombe priest o.m.i. (page 52)

Hamelin, Angelique: B-47, Angelique Hamelin, baptized 17 December 1859, age about 10 days, daughter of Pierre Hamelin and Marianne Makkomitekkwe, Godmother: Angelique L'Hyrondelle, Albert Lacombe priest o.m.i. (page 17)

Hamelin, Eustache: B-9, Eustache Hamelin, baptized 21 July 1872, age one month, illegitimate son of Eustache Hamelin and Marie Desjarlais, Godfather: Eustache Berard, Godmother: Marguerite Primeau, J. Joseph Dupuis priest o.m.i. (page 78)

Hamelin, Henri: B-15, Henri Hamelin, baptized 12 [?] December 1890, born 5 .., son of Charles Hamelin and Nancy Deschamps, Godfather: Pierre Ladue, Godmother: Mrs. .., L. Fouquet omi. (page 140)

Hamelin, Jeanne: B-29, Jeanne Hamelin, baptized 28 May 1859, age 4 months 5 days, legitimate daughter of Charles Hamelin and Therese Courteoreille, Godfather: Louis Bouvet, Godmother: Jeanne Kakeisik [?], C. M. Frain m.o.m.i. (page 13)

Hammelin, Nancy: B-37, Nancy Hammelin, baptized 27 January 1861 at Fort Montagne, age 5 months, daughter of Charles Hammelin and Therese Courteoreille, Godfather: Jean Baptiste Anas, Godmother: Catherine Cardinal, Alb. Lacombe priest o.m.i. (page 26-27)

Hamelin, Samuel: B-16, Samuel Hamelin, baptized 7 October 1888, born 30 September 1888, of the legitimate marriage of Charles Hamelin and Nancy Deschamps, Godmother: Nancy Sapin dite Campion, J. J. M. Lestanc priest o.m.i. (page 126)

Hammelin, Sophie: B-149, Sophie Hammelin, baptized 31 May 1863, age 9 months, daughter of Joseph Hammelin and Marie Louise Laurence, Godfather: Louis Fontaine, Godmother: Marie Atakkokek, J. M. Caer o.m.i. priest. (page 52)

Hamelin, William: B-1, William Hamelin, baptized 22 January 1890, born 19 January 1890, of Charles Hamelin and Nancy Deschamps, Godfather: La Frambois Ward, Godmother: Nancy Campion, L. Fouquet o.m.i. (page 133)

Hamilton, William and Veronique Dumont: M-4, William Hamilton, son of the late John Hamilton and Amelia Payne, married 11 December 1888, Veronique Dumont, legitimate daughter of the late Jacques Dumont and the late Marie-Anne Bruneau, Present: Jane Gibbons (signed), P. Bowez (signed), H. Grandin o.m.i. (page 127)

Hanihanis, Isabelle: B-94, Isabelle Hanihanis, baptized 31 December 1861, age one month, daughter of Michel Hanihanis and Isabelle Godin, Godfather: Pierre Dumond, Godmother: Rosalie Goin, P. Caer o.m.i. (page 39)

Hanihanis, Nancy: S-3, Nancy Hanihanis, buried 21 January 1861, age 17 years, wife of Louis Lebrun, Present: Olivier Laderoute and Alexis Bruneau, Alb. Lacombe priest o.m.i. (page 26)

Hebert, Bazile and Angelique Vallee: M-5, Bazile Hebert, adult son of Pierre Hebert and Agathe Vanasse, married 24 October 1861, Angelique Vallee, widow of Louis Leblanc, Present: Dosithe Sicard dit Carifel and Rev. Father Caer (signed), Alb. Lacombe priest o.m.i. (page 38)

Hebert, Marie Salome: B-95, Marie Salome Hebert, baptized 2 January 1862, born 30 December 1861, daughter of Bazile Hebert and Angelique Vallee, Godfather: Dosithe Sicard dit Carifel, Godmother: Henriette LeBlanc, Alb. Lacombe priest o.m.i. (page 40)

Holland, Frederick: B-3, Frederick Holland, baptized 22 January 1886, age 9 days, son of John Holland and Marie Short, H. Grandin o.m.i. (page 110)

Holland, Jesse Joseph: B-14, Jesse Joseph Holland, baptized 27 October 1890, born 17 October 1890 at Edmonton, son of John Holland and Mary (born Short), Godfather: Pachal Xavier Marshal (signed), Godmother: his wife, Archange, L. Fouquet priest. (page 139)

Hudson, Albert: B-113, Albert Hudson, May 1862, age 4 months, son of Georges Hudson and Mary Roland, Godmother: Sophie Chatelain, Albert Lacombe priest o.m.i. (page 43)

Hudson, Albert: S-9, Albert Hudson, buried 15 January 1863, age one year, son of Georges Hudson and Mary Rolland, Witnesses: Henri Paquet and Jean Baptiste Courtepatte, Alb. Lacombe priest o.m.i. (page 46)

Hudson, Henry: B-154, Henry Hudson, baptized 22 January 1864, born yesterday, son of George Hudson and Mary Rowland, Godfather: Richard Colin, Godmother: Jeanne Folley, Alb. Lacombe priest o.m.i. (page 53)

Hudson, James: B-2, James Hudson, baptized 23 January 1858, age 2 days, son of George Hudson and Marie Roland, Godfather: James Short, Godmother: Louise Bouvet, A. Lacombe priest. o.m.i. (page 1)

Hudson, Marie: B-27, Marie Hudson, baptized 14 April 1859, born today, daughter of Georges Hudson and Marie Rowland, Godfather: James Richard, Godmother: Judith Godin, C. M. Frain m.o.m.i. (page 13)

Hudson, William: S-2, William Hudson, buried 10 January 1859, age 11 years, son of George Hudson and Marie Rowland, Witnesses: Antoine Galarneau, Michel Kalliou, and Augustin Auger, A. Lacombe priest o.m.i. (page 9)

Iamiywtakuskew, Joseph [or Famiywtakuskew]: B-30, Joseph Iamiywtakuskew, baptized 8 May 1859, age one month, son of Iamiywtakuskew and Lisette Courteoreille, Godfather: Joseph Courteoreille, Godmother: Sophie Peysimouwop, C. M. Frain m.o.m.i. (page 13)

Inkster, Annie: See James Norris and Annie Inkster

Iyakwapistam, Pierre: B-48, Pierre Iyakwapistam, baptized 17 September 1858, age one months, son of Iyakwapistam and Kwaninin, Godmother: Angelique Crise, A. Lacombe priest o.m.i. (page 7)

Johnson, Frank and Genevieve Duquet: M-4, Frank Johnson, adult son of Johny Johnson and Marie Clement, married 12 May 1859, Genevieve Duquet, minor daughter of __ Duquet and a Sauteuse, Witnesses: Basyl Hubert, Pierre St.Sauveur and Pierre Pearson, C. M. Frain m.o.m.i. (page 14)

Johnson, Maggy: B-5, Maggy Johnson, baptized 21 March 1886, born yesterday, (illegitimate) of William Johnson and Rosalie Berard, Godfather: .., Godmother: Julie Dagneau, H. Grandin o.m.i. (page 110)

Kaapisisit, Antoine: B-133, Antoine Kaapisisit, baptized 8 August 1863, age one year, son of Kaapisisit and Kiskanakwas, Godfather: Antoine Savard, Godmother: Marie Tastawitch, Alb. Lacombe priest o.m.i. (page 48)

Kaayattowe, Jean Baptiste: B-138, Jean Baptiste Kaayattowe, baptized 17 August 1863, age one month, son of Kaayattowe and Nawikkikabow [?], Godmother: Marie Belanger, Alb. Lacombe priest o.m.i. (page 49)

Kabawis, Marie: B-84, Marie Kabawis, baptized 23 July 1861, age 19 days, daughter of Jacques Kabawis and Susanne Iskwese, Godfather: Gabriel Dumond, J. Caer o.m.i. (page 36)

Kabawis, Pierre: B-51, Pierre Kabawis, baptized 2 October 1858, age one months, son of Albert Kabawis and Henriette Awikas, Godmother: Suzanne Opimuttawis, A. Lacombe priest o.m.i. (page 7)

Kabawis, Sophie: B-10, Sophie Kabawis, baptized 24 January 1859, age 8 days, daughter of Jacques Kabawis and Suzanne Iskwes, Godmother: Otayamiwis, A. Lacombe priest o.m.i. (page 10)

Kabawis, Sophie: B-17, Sophie Kabawis, baptized 29 September 1871, age 10 days, daughter of Jacques Kabawis and Catherine Cris, Godfather: Eustache Berard, Godmother: Marguerite Primeau, Alb. Lacombe priest o.m.i. (page 76)

Kadawastak, James: B-3, James (Kadawastak), baptized 11 February 1883, age one week, son of Louise Kakawastak, Godmother: Josephte Crise, C. Scollen priest o.m.i. (page 87)

Kakipasiko, Albert: B-40, Albert Kakipasiko, baptized 30 September 1859, age 2 months, son of Antoine Kakipasiko and Rosalie Bruno, Godmother: Mary Rowland, C. M. Frain o.m.i. (page 16)

Kakipasiko, Eloiza: B-112, Eloiza Kakipasiko, baptized 1 October 1862, age one months, daughter of Antoine Kakipasiko and Rosalie Bruneault, Godfather: Antoine Lebrun, Godmother: Isabelle Bruneault, Alb. Lacombe priest o.m.i. (page 43)

Kakkawayis, Sophie: B-3, Sophie Kakkawayis, baptized 26 January 1858, age one month, daughter of Kakkawayis and Angelique, Godfather: Jean Baptiste Peyesimwop, A. Lacombe priest o.m.i. (page 1)

Kakwatshitta, Jean Baptiste: B-49, Jean Baptiste Kakwatshitta, bt. 26 Feb 1861, age 2 years, s/o Kakwatshitta and Rosalie Dion, Gm: Angelique Cardinal, Alb. Lacombe ptre o.m.i. (page 29)

Kalliou, Adelaide: B-3, Adelaide Kalliou, baptized 11 January 1859, born today, of Michel Kalliou and Marie Savard, Godfather: Louis Larence, Godmother: Marguerite Kalliou, A. Lacombe priest o.m.i. (page 9)

Kalliou, Eliza: B-153, Eliza Kalliou, baptized 27 September 1863, born yesterday, daughter of Michel Kalliou and Marie Savard, Godfather: Benjamin St.Arnauld, Godmother: Josephte Bellecourt, Alb. Lacombe priest o.m.i. (page 52-53)

Kalliou, Francois Xavier: B-25, Francois Xavier Kalliou, baptized 26 January 1860, born yesterday, legitimate son of Thomas Kalliou and Marie Fineley, Godfather: John Cunningham (signed), Godmother: Josephte Bellecourt, C. M. Fran p.o.m.i. (page 23)

Kalliou, Francois Xavier: S-4, Francois Xavier Kalliou, buried 30 July 1861, age over one year, son of Thomas Kalliou and Mary Finlay, Witnesses: Baptiste Courtepatte and John Cunningham (signed), Alb. Lacombe priest o.m.i. (page 35-36)

Kalliou, Johny: B-27, Johny Kalliou, baptized 12 March 1860, age over one month, legitimate son of Baptiste Kalliou and Angelique Bruno, Godfather: George Hatson [Hudson], Godmother: Marie Rolland, C. M. Frain o.m.i. (page 24)

Kalliou, William: B-122, William Kalliou, baptized 27 December 1862, born yesterday, son of Thomas Kalliou and Marie Fineley, Godfather: William Kalliou, Godmother: Nancy, J. M. Caer priest o.m.i. (page 45)

Kamikkatawokap, Ema: B-47, Ema Kamikkatawokap, baptized 24 February 1861, age 3 years, daughter of the deceased Kamikkatawokap and Lisette daughter of the deceased Mistakaw, Godfather: Louis Piche, Alb. Lacombe priest o.m.i. (page 28)

Kamikwakanel, Genevieve: B-164, Genevieve Kamikwakanel baptized 4 September 1864, age about 30 years, Godfather: Richard Dick, Godmother: Genevieve Bruyere, M. R. Remas o.m.i. priest. (page 55)

Kamikweskwewew, Alexis and Bethy: M-3, Alexis Kamikweskwewew, catholic, married 15 June 1873, Bethy, protestant, Witnesses: Samuel Cunningham and Bazile Larence, J. Joseph Dupuis priest o.m.i. (page 81)

Kaminakus, Jerome: B-7, Jerome Kaminakus, baptized 23 January 1859, age 4 months, son of Kaminakus and Akines, Godmother: __ Petaskewisk, A. Lacombe priest o.m.i. (page 10)

Kamistatimopikiskwe, Louis: B-17, Louis Kamistatimopikiskwe, baptized 11 January 1860, age 4 months, son of Kamistatimopikiskwe and Josephte Mindito, Godfather: Louis Batoche, Albert Lacombe priest o.m.i. (page 22)

Kamiyokwaneb, Genevieve: B-8, Genevieve Kamiyokwaneb, baptized 23 January 1859, age 10 months, daughter of Kamiyokwaneb and Genevieve Pepamwewitam, Godmother: Otayemiwis, A. Lacombe priest o.m.i. (page

St.Joachim, Fort Auguste (Fort Edmonton) 1858-1890

Kamiyotakuskew, Victor: B-158, Victor Kamiyotakuskew, baptized 27 March 1864, age 35 years, Godfather: Abraham Salois, Godmother: Jane Finlay, M. R. Remas priest o.m.i. (page 54)

Kamiyotakuskew, Victor: M-9, Victor Kamiyotakuskew, married 27 March 1864, Lisette Courte-oreille, Present: Abraham Salois and James Finlay, M. R. Remas priest o.m.i. (page 54)

Kanayawatasiw, Jean-Marie and Marie Kanaweyim: M-1, Jean-Marie Kanayawatasiw married 30 January 1859 Marie Kanaweyim, Witnesses: Albert Rabawis and Louis Piche, A. Lacombe priest o.m.i. (page 12)

Kanamattiw, Thomas: B-157, Thomas Kanamattiw, baptized 17 March 1864, age about 6 months, son of Kanamattiw and Mokkakup, Godfather: Richard Colin, M. R. Remas priest o.m.i. (page 53)

Kapistowesit, Marie: B-105, Marie Kapistowesit, baptized 1 April 1862, age 6 years, daughter of Kapistowesit and Petaskewisk, Godfather: Louis Piche, Alb. Lacombe priest o.m.i. (page 42)

Kapotet, Michel: B-44, Michel Kapotet, baptized 16 September 1858, age one month, son of Pierre Kapotet [Ledoux] and Magdeleine Deslauriers (Desnoyers), Godfather: Edouard Genereux, Godmother: Marguerite Des Jardins, C. M. Frain m.o.m.i. (page 6)

Karakonti, Bernard: M-3, Bernard Karakonti, widower of Marie (Iroquois), married 9 November 1868, Judith, minor daughter of Anne Nijatens, Present: __ Berreau and Catherine Bellerose, V. Vegreville. (page 66)

Kasekkotchakwe, Agathe: B-26, Agathe Kasekkotchakwe, baptized 7 February 1858, age two years, daughter of Kasekkotchakwe and Kuayakosimo, Godfather: Alexys Cardinal, A. Lacombe priest o.m.i. (page 4)

Kasiwekasette, Isaac: B-13, Isaac Kasiwekasette, baptized 11 January 1860, age about 7 years, son of the deceased Kasiwekasette and Oskases, Godfather: Jean-Baptiste Courtepatte, Albert Lacombe priest o.m.i. (page 21)

Kasokkatshakwe, Felix: B-18, Felix Kasokkatshakwe, baptized 13 January 1860, age 6 months, son of Kasokkatshakwe and Ayakusinew, Godmother: Charlotte Kasokkatshakwe, Albert Lacombe priest o.m.i. (page 22)

Kekkek, Noel: B-1, Noel Kekkek, baptized 1 January 1858, age 2 months, son of Kekkek and Marianne Crisse, Godmother: Marie Savard, A. Lacombe priest o.m.i. (page 1)

Kekipasiko, Susanne: B-3, Susanne Kekipasiko, baptized 29 March 1868, born yesterday, son of Antoine Kekipasiko and Rosalie Bruneault, Godfather: George McDougall (signed John George McDougald), Godmother: Susanne Kawittakkyik, Alb. Lacombe priest o.m.i. (page 64)

34

Kelly, Catherine: See Davis McNaught and Catherine Kelly

Kelly, Charles: Charles Kelly, March 1885 confirmation, H. Grandin o.m.i. (page 104)

Kelly, Elizabeth: See Stanislas Larue and Elizabeth Kelly

Kelly, John Albert: B-8, John Albert Kelly, baptized 17 May 1888, born yesterday, of the legitimate marriage of John Kelly and Georgiana Foisy, Godfather: Stanislas Sauve (signed), Godmother: Agnes Kelly, (signed), H. Grandin o.m.i. (page 124)

Kelly, John George Edmund: B-17, John George Edmund Kelly, baptized 2 September 1886, born this morning, of the legitimate marriage of John Edmond Kelly and Georgiane Foisy, Godfather: George Roy, Godmother: Elizabeth Kelly, H. Grandin o.m.i. (page 115)

Kelly, Mary Ann: B-9, Mary Ann Kelly, baptized 19 [?] June 1890, born 15 June 1890, legitimate daughter of John Kelly (signed) and Georgiana (born Foissy), Godfather: Luk Kelly, Godmother: Margaret Kelly, L. Fouquet priest. (page 137)

Kelly, Mary Brene: B-9, Mary Brene Kelly, baptized 20 July 1889, born yesterday, of the legitimate marriage of Luke Kelly and Elisa Lapagerie, Godfather: Joseph Picard, Godmother: Marguerite Lapagerie, V. Vegreville o.m.i. (page 130)

Kelly, William: William Kelly, March 1885 confirmation, H. Grandin o.m.i. (page 104)

Ketoweyakis, Therese: B-4, Therese Ketoweyakis, baptized 26 January 1858, age 7 months, daughter of Ketowayakis and Ayalemkwepiw [?], Godfather: Albert Kabawis, Godmother: Henriette Awikas, A. Lacome priest o.m.i. (page 1)

Kettewasakay, Josephte: B-21, Josephte Kettewasakay, baptized 30 January 1859, age about 80 years, daughter of Kettewasakay, Godfather: Pierre Kyikawakabew, A. Lacombe priest o.m.i. (page 11)

Kinikapiwin, Marie: B-28, Marie Kinikapiwin, baptized 26 March 1858, age 4 months, daughter of Kinikapiwin and Omanukkwe, Godfather: Charles Dumet, Godmother: Marie St.Arnaud, A. Lacombe priest o.m.i. (page 4)

Kinikapiwiyin, Alexis: B-46, Alexis Kinikapiwiyin, baptized 24 February 1861, age one year, son of Kinikapiwiyin and Onahakitohikamikwe, Godfather: Alexis Cardinal, Alb. Lacombe priest o.m.i. (page 28)

Kistinaham, Angelique: B-4, Angelique Kistinaham, baptized 29 June 1865, age about 25 years, daughter of Kistinaham, Godfather: Samuel Cunningham (signed), Godmother: Angelique L'Hyrondelle, Alb. Lacombe priest o.m.i. (page 60)

St.Joachim, Fort Auguste (Fort Edmonton) 1858-1890

Kitiskwewin, Marie: B-2, Marie Kitiskwewin, baptized 7 January 1872, Joseph Dupuis priest o.m.i. (page 76)

Kisikawokabew, Nancy: B-1, Nancy Kisikawokabew, baptized 5 January 1860, age 6 days, daughter of Pierre Kisikawokabew and Catherine Sesesiw, Godfather: Alexis Naud, Albert Lacombe priest o.m.i. (page 19)

Komikwasiwaniw, Jean Marie: B-15, Jean Marie Komikwasiwaniw, baptized 11 January 1860, age 2 months, son of Komikwasiwaniw and Marguerite Piyeta, Godfather: Jean-Baptiste Courtepatte, Albert Lacombe priest o.m.i. (page 21)

Kwanes/Kwenes/Kwinis

Kwinis, Johny and Julie Nisothesis: M-10, Johny Kwinis, married 27 March 1864, Julie Nisothesis, Present: Pierre St.Sauveur and Antoine Savard, M. R. Remas priest o.m.i. (page 54)

Kwanes, Olivier: B-9, Olivier Kwanes, baptized 15 August 1869, age one month, of Johny Kwanes and ... [?], Godfather: Olivier Bellerose, V. Bourgine priest. (page 69)

Kwenes, Paul: B-_, Paul Kwenes, baptized 10 November 1866, born 3 November, of the legitimate marriage of Jean Kwenes and Julie Wapens, Godfather: Norbert Belrose, Godmother: Josette Savard, A. Andre o.m.i. priest. (page 62-63)

Kwenis, Veronique: B-4, Veronique Kwenis, baptized 11 April 1869, age 2 days, daughter of Charles Kwenis and Jany Stevenson, Godfather: Olivier Bellerose, Godmother: Catherine Surprenant, V. Bourgine priest. (page 67)

L'hirondelle, J. Baptiste and Euphrosine Beauregard: M-1, J. Baptiste L'hirondelle, of Lac Ste. Anne, married 27 January 1873, Euphrosine Beauregard, Witnesses: J. B. Divertissant and Joseph Paquette [?], J. Joseph Dupuis priest o.m.i. (page 80)

L'Hyrondelle, Flora: B-24, Flora L'Hyrondelle, baptized 10 August 1883, age 8 days, daughter of Albert L'Hyrondelle and Anne Gladu, Godfather: Edouard Durocher, Godmother: Marguerite Gladu, H. J. H. Blais priest o.m.i. (page 92)

Laderoute, Anne: B-37, Anne Laderoute, baptized 25 July 1858, age 10 days, daughter of Olivier Seguin Laderoute and Angelique L'Hyrondelle, Godfather: Pierre L'Hyrondelle, Godmother: Angelique L'Hyrondelle, A. Lacombe priest o.m.i. (page 5)

Laderoute, Francois Seguin: B-74, Francois Seguin dit Laderoute, baptized 4 April 1861, born today, son of Olivier Seguin dit Laderoute and Angelique L'Hyrondelle, Godfather: Jean Baptiste Courteoreille, Godmother: Josephte Bellecourt, J. M. St. Caer priest o.m.i. (page 33-34)

St.Joachim, Fort Auguste (Fort Edmonton) 1858-1890

Ladouceur, Eloiza: B-33, Eloiza Ladouceur, baptized 27 June 1859, age 27 days, daughter of Pierre Ladouceur and Marguerite Fraser, Godfather: Jean Baptiste Anas, Godmother: Catherine Cardinal, A. Lacombe priest o.m.i.

LaFerte, Jean Baptiste: S-3, Jean Baptiste LaFerte, buried 31 May 1859, died yesterday, age about 38 years, Witnesses: Pierre Pearson, Xavier Lepine, and Baptiste Courtepatte, C. M. Frain m.o.m.i. (page 14)

Lafreniere, Ambroise: B-33, Ambroise Lafreniere, baptized 6 September 1860, born 6 January, legitimate son of Francis Lafreniere and Isabelle St.Germain, Godfather: Baptiste Lafreniere, Godmother: Ursule St.Germain, J. M. St. Caer [?] o.m.i. (page 25)

Lagraine, Baptiste and Morisis: M-4, Baptiste Lagraine, son of Baptiste Lagraine and Kateyayeyisk, married 10 September 1885, Morisis, daughter of Miyawicakes and Maggy, Present: Martin Divertissant and Pierish Cardinal, H. Grandin o.m.i. (page 107)

Landry, Marianne: B-117, Marianne Landry, baptized 11 May 1862, age 3 months, daughter of Alexandre Landry and Marie Testawitch, Godfather: Bazile Laurence, Godmother: Marianne Gaudry, Alb. Lecombe priest o.m.i. (page 44)

Lapatate, Mary: B-7, Mary Lapatate, baptized 28 March 1884, daughter of Lapatate, Godfather: H. Grandin, C. Scollen priest o.m.i. (page 97)

Larant, Isabelle: B-11, Isabelle Larant, baptized 21 July 1886, born yesterday of the legitimate marriage of Adam Larant and Peggy Lagrave, Godfather: Joseph Gouin, Godmother: Caroline Vivier, H. Grandin o.m.i. (page 112)

Larocque/Laroque

Larocque, Caroline: B-17, Caroline Larocque, baptized 29 October 1888, born 20 October 1888, of the legitimate marriage of Louis Larocque and Angelique Sauve, Godmother: Mrs. Boudeau [?] Godfather: Benj. Boudeau [?], H. Grandin o.m.i. (page 126)

Laroque, Charles: B-12, Charles Laroque, baptized 9 August 1890, born _, of Louis Laroque and Angelique Sauve, Godfather: Mr. Vozina, Godmother: _ Laroque, L. Fouquet o.m.i. (page 138)

Larocque, Clara Marie: B-11, Clara Marie Larocque, baptized 6 [?] May 1885, age 17 days, legitimate daughter of Louis Laroque and Angelique Sauve, Godfather: Alexis Desgagne, Godmother: Marie wife of Johnny Paul, H. Grandin o.m.i. (page 105-106)

Larocque, Edward: B-2, Edward Larocque, baptized 24 January 1887, born 7 January 1887, of the legitimate marriage of Louis Larocque and Angelique Sauve, Godmother: Veronique Ayamikaya, H. Grandin o.m.i. (page 119)

Larocque, Francois and Marianne Pattenaude: M-8, Francois Larocque, minor son of Francois Larocque and Angelique Crise, married 20 July 1863, Marianne Pattenaude, minor daughter of Jean Baptiste Pattenaude and Felicite Arcand, Witnesses: Pierre Beauchamp and Charles Racette, Alb. Lacombe pte o.m.i. (page 47)

Laroque, James: B-20, James Laroque, baptized 11 July 1883, age 2 weeks, son of Louis Laroque and Angelique Sauve, Godfather: Louis Hamelin, Godmother: Ellen his wife, C. Scollen priest o.m.i. (page 91)

Larocque, Joseph Manitowikyik: B-152, Joseph Manitowikyik (Larocque), baptized 27 September 1863, age about one month, son of Pierre Larocque Manitowikyik and Marie Pinaud (Mayikikabow), Godmother: Susanne Makkonutekkwe, Alb. Lacombe priest o.m.i. (page 52)

Larocque, Joseph Manitowikyik: B-18, Joseph Manitowekijik Larocque, baptized 15 October 1871, age about 20 days, of the legitimate marriage of Pierre Manitowekijik and Marie Mayokabaing, Godfather: Joseph Paquet, H. Leduc o.m.i. priest. (page 76)

Laroque, Marie Rose: B-2, Marie Rose Laroque, baptized 7 February 1875, born 3 February 1875, legitimate daughter of Louis Laroque and Angelique Sauve, Godfather: Mathias, Godmother: Peggy Leslie, V. Vegreville p. o.m.i. (page 86)

Larocque, Pierre Manitowikyik: B-6, Pierre Manitowikyik Larocque, baptized 21 January 1859, age 10 months, son of Pierre Manitowikyik Larocque and Marie Mayitikabaw Pinaud, Godfather: Marie Awinal, A. Lacombe priest o.m.i. (page 10)

Larue, Stanislas and Elizabeth Kelly: M-3, Stanislas Larue, legitimate adult son of Stanislas Larue and Aguelline Bitournay, married 27 November 1888, Elizabeth Kelly, legitimate adult daughter of the late William Kelly and Margaret Harney, Present: Geo. Roy (signed) and Antoine Prince (signed), Agnes Kelly (signed), L. K. Kelly (signed), H. Grandin o.m.i. (page 127)

Laurence/Laurance

Laurance, Ambroise: B-130, Ambroise Laurance, baptized 8 August 1863, age 2 months, son of Bazile Laurance and Marguerite Desjardins, Godfather: Ambroise Petitbriand (Durocher), Godmother: Catherine [..], Albert Lacombe priest o.m.i. (page 47-48)

Laurence, Florence: B-11, Florence Laurence, born and baptized 6 February 1871, of the legitimate marriage of Bazile Laurence and Marguerite, his wife, Godfather: Francois Deschamps, Godmother: Catherine Brunault, Bourgine priest. (page 74)

Laurence, Julie: B-10, Julie Laurence, baptized 6 September 1874, age 15 days, daughter of Basil Laurence and Marguerite Desjarlais, Godfather: Johny Laurence, Godmother: Julie Dagnon, Constantin .... priest o.m.i. (page 84)

Laurence, Louis and Olive Bellerose: M-1, Louis Laurence, minor son of Bazile Laurence and Agathe Kalliou, married 24 September 1860, Olive Bellerose, minor daughter of Olivier Bellerose and Josephte Savard, Pressent: Olivier Bellerose, Michel Kalliou, and Thomas Kalliou, Alb. Lacombe priest o.m.i. (page 25)

Laurance, Victor: B-97, Victor Laurance, baptized 15 March 1862, age 8 days, son of the deceased Louis Laurance and Olive Bellerose, Godfather: Benjamin Bellerose, Godmother: Marie Bellerose, Alb. Lacombe priest o.m.i. (page 40)

Leblanc, Victoire: B-32, Victoire Leblanc, baptized 13 May 1858, age 2 years, daughter of Louis Leblanc and Angelique Vallee, Godfather: Felix Monro, Godmother: Isabelle Lucier, A. Lacombe priest o.m.i. (page 5)

Lebrun, Abraham: B-12, Abraham Lebrun, born and baptized 11 February 1871, of the legitimate marriage of Pierre Lebrun and Catherine Lapatate, his wife, Godfather: Pierre Deschenaux, Godmother: Caroline __, Bourgine priest. (page 74)

Lebrun, Abraham (Maikosis): B-15, Abraham Lebrun, born and baptized 11 February 1871, of the legitimate marriage of Pierre Lebrun (Maikosis) and Catherine Lapatate, Godfather: Pierre Deschenaux, Godmother: Caroline Courchaine, A. Andre o.m.i. priest. (page 75) [This entry is crossed out.]

Lebrun, Felix: S-12, Felix Lebrun, buried 26 December 1864, age one year, son of Pierre Lebrun and Catherine Anhanis, Witnesses: Louis Roussel and Bruno Piyesimwop [Petit-Couteau], Alb. Lacombe priest o.m.i. (page 58)

Lebrun, Marie: S-4, Marie Lebrun, buried 27 June 1859, age 14 years, daughter of Pierre Lebrun and Marie Piednoir, Witnesses: Felix Monroe and Georges Hatson, A. Lacombe priest o.m.i. (page 14)

Lebrun, Narcisse: B-40, Narcisse Lebrun, baptized 2 February 1861, age one month, son of Louis Lebrun and Nancy Hanihanis, Godfather: Thomas Boucher, Godmother: Marie Hanihanis, J. M. St. Caer [?] o.m.i. (page 27)

Lebrun, Olivier Mayikosis: B-5, Olivier Mayikosis (Lebrun), baptized 20 July 1868, born 17 July, of the legitimate marriage of Pierre Mayikosis and Catherine Ahniyanis, Godfather: Olivier Bellerose, Godmother: Josephte Courtepatte, H. Leduc priest o.m.i. (page 65)

Lebrun, Paul and Nancy: M-2, Paul Lebrun, married 1 May 1883, Nancy, orphan protegee of Johnny Paul, Witnesses: Jos. Paul and Philomene, C. Scollen priest. o.m.i. (page 90)

St.Joachim, Fort Auguste (Fort Edmonton) 1858-1890

Lebrun, Pierre and Catherine Anehanes: M-3, Pierre Lebrun, minor son of Pierre Lebrune, married 28 February 1859, Catherine Anehanes, minor daughter of Anehanes and Josephte Lawenlee [?], Present: Antoine Galarneau and Antoine Auger, M. R. Remas p.o.m.i. (page 12)

Lemire, Clotilde: B-5, Clotilde Lemire, baptized 15 December 1870, born yesterday, of the legitimate marriage of Francois Lemire and Suzanne Boucher, Godfather: Pierre Deschamps and his wife, V. Bourgine priest. (page 70)

Logan, Albert Edward: B-11, Albert Edward Logan, baptized 3 April 1883, son of Nathaniel Logan and Sarah Page, Godfather: Moise Page, Godmother: Marie, wife of J. Norris, C. Scollen priest o.m.i. (page 89)

Mac, Nancy: B-139, Nancy Mac, baptized 17 August 1863, age one year, daughter of the deceased Joseph Mac and Paskwawiskwe, Godmother: Marie Boucher, Alb. Lacombe priest o.m.i. (page 49)

MacIvor, Donald and Angelique Cardinal: M-9, Donald MacIvor, adult son of Allen MacIvor and Elisabeth Beeds, married 28 June 1884, Angelique Cardinal, adult daughter of the late Andre Cardinal and Rosalie Breland, J. Joseph Dupuis priest. (page 98-99)

Maklianis, Simon and Henry: B-7 and B-8, Simon and Henry Maklianis, baptized 22 May 1886, Simon age 2 years and Henry age over 2 months, son ofs of Paul Maklianis and Josephte, Godmother: Rosalie, H. Grandin o.m.i. (page 111)

Maminowatam, Pierre: B-7, Pierre Maminowatam, baptized 2 February 1858, age 3 years, son of Maminowatam and Ema, Godmother: Eloise Domatas, A. Lacombe priest o.m.i. (page 2)

Maninawataw, Agnes: B-3, Agnes Maninawataw, baptized 24 January 1871, age 2 months, of the marriage of Maninawataw and Emma, Godfather: James Laurence, Godmother: Marie Boucher, V. Bourgine priest. (page 72)

Maskegon, Julien Marie: B-35, Julien Marie Maskegon, baptized 18 September 1859, born 12 September, legitimate son of Henri Maskegon and Suzanne Courteoreille, Godfather: Baptiste Robertson, Godmother: Marie St.Arnaud, C. M. Frain m.o.m.i. (page 15)

Maskikiwinaken, Marie: B-19, Marie Maskikiwinaken, baptized 25 January 1859, age 6 months, daughter of Maskikiwinaken and Marie Maskwatapinenttet, Godfather: Pierre Kipkawakabow, A. Lacombe priest o.m.i. (page 11)

Maskikwinakus, Alexis: B-67, Alexis Maskikwinakus, baptized 3 March 1861, age 2 years, son of Maskikwinakus and Wabikkewes, Godfather: Alexis Okimawasis, Alb. Lacombe priest o.m.i. (page 32)

Maskitattakwan, Catherine: B-23, Catherine Maskitattakwan, baptized 17 January 1860, age 6 months, daughter of Maskitattakwan and Kwatshitat, Godfather: Alexis Okionawasis, Albert Lacombe priest o.m.i. (page 23)

Maskwa, Eliza: B-10, Eliza Maskwa, baptized 2 August 1884, age 4 months, daughter of Maskwa and Peutawew, H. Grandin o.m.i. (page 99)

Matchiyas, James: B-21, James Matchiyas, baptized 22 July 1883, age 3 weeks, son of Matchiyas and Jannette Crise, Godfather: James Norris, C. Scollen priest o.m.i. (page 92)

Matsuskisk, Clara: B-2, Clara Matsuskisk, baptized 16 March 1890, age 20 days, daughter of Jeannotte Matsuskisk, Godmother: Marie-Rose Belanger, V. Vegreville o.m.i. (page 133)

Maurcou, Elisabeth: B-6, Elisabeth Maurcou, baptized 14 June 1874, age 5 days, daughter of Antoine Maurcou and Marguerite Isisawan, Godfather: Thomas Desjarlais, Godmother: Elisabeth wife of Arnaud, J. Joseph Dupuis priest o.m.i. (page 83)

Maurereau [Maurcou], Antoine and Marguerite Isisawan or Watiskan: M-1, Antoine Maurereau [Maurcou?], married 28 June 1874, Marguerite Isisawan or Watiskan, Witnesses: Henri Paquet Sr., Antoine Paquet, M. Bellerore, J. Joseph Dupuis priest o.m.i. (page 84)

McDonald/MacDonald

MacDonald, Alexandre: B-3, Alexandre MacDonald, baptized 1 March 1885, age 14 days, son of William MacDonald and Nancy Hamelin, Godmother: Cecile Nabes, H. Grandin o.m.i. (page 104)

McDonald, Angus and Angelique Briand: M-1, Angus McDonald, widower of Angelique Laurence, married 22 February 1871, Angelique Briand, minor daughter of Philippe Briand and Magdelaine Chatelin (written above Catherine Parant), Witnesses: Ambroise Briand and Andrew Favel, A. Andre o.m.i. priest. (page 74-75)

McDonald, Marie: See David Saint-Clair and Marie McDonald

MacDowell, Catherine: See Donald MacLean and Catherine Mac Dowell

MacKenney, Mary Marguerite: B-4, Mary Marguerite MacKenney, baptized 21 March 1886, age 14 days, daughter of William MacKenney and Magy, Godmother: Veronique Dumont, Godfather: Johny Paul, H. Grandin o.m.i. (page 110)

McKenney, William James: B-9, William James McKenney, baptized 1 April 1883, age one month, son of William McKenney and Marguerite, Godfather: Bernard Iroquois, Godmother: Julie, wife of James Rowland, C. Scollen priest o.m.i. (page 88)

St.Joachim, Fort Auguste (Fort Edmonton) 1858-1890

McLean, Catherine: B-13, Catherine McLean, baptized 6 October 1889, born 10 September 1889, legitimate daughter of Donald McLean and Melanie Cardinal, Godfather: Norman Vandale, Godmother: Julie McGillis, V. Vegreville o.m.i. (page 131)

MacLean, Donald and Catherine Mac Dowell: M-1, Donald MacLean (signed with and x), son of John MacLean and Catherine Mac Dowell, married 23 May 1888, Melanie Cardinal, daughter of the late St.Luc Cardinal and Marguerite Desjarlais, Witnesses: V. Degagne and E. D...., H. Grandin o.m.i. (page 124)

McLean, Jean: B-15, Jean McLean, baptized 17 January 1888, born yesterday, of the legitimate marriage of Donald Mac Lean and Melanie Cardinal, Godmother: Mrs. Isabelle Laframboise, H. Grandin o.m.i. (married Maria Laderoute 7 March 19.., St.Paul des Metis) (page 126)

McNaught, Davis and Catherine Kelly: M-1, Davis McNaught (signed D. McNaught), adult son of John McNaught and Elisa McCrossen, of Sussex, New Brunswick, married 31 October 1889, Catherine Kelly (signed Katie Kelly), adult daughter of the late William Kelly and Marguerite Harney [or Harvey], of Alexandria Ontario, Present: Joseph Kelly (signed), Agnes Kelly (signed), Luke Kelly (signed), S. LeRue (signed), V. Vegreville o.m.i. (page 132)

Meaver/Maver/Mayver

Maver, Anne: B-7, Anne Maver [Meaver], baptized 13 September 1868, age one month, daughter of Maver William [William Meaver] and Jeanny Folly (Gladu), Godmother: Marie Kissenatisiwop, Alb. Lacombe priest o.m.i. (page 65)

Mayver, Henry: B-16, Henri Mayver, baptized 11 July 1871, born one month of Mayver and Jennie Gladu, his "concubiuage", Godfather: Henri Paquette, Godmother: Euphrosine Beausayer, A. Blanchet priest. (page 75)

Meskey, Pierre: B-10, Pierre Meskey, baptized 13 July 1873, age .. and 4 months, son of Francois Meskey and Marguerite Pafraniwes [?], Godfather: Pierre Lebrun, Godmother: Therese Berland, J. Joseph Dupuis priest o.m.i. (page 81)

Mikkopiesiw, Joseph: B-5, Joseph Mikkopiesiw, baptized 20 January 1858, age 10 months, son of Nikkopiesiw and Mittawikihat, Godfather: Joseph Piesimwop, Godmother: Sophie Piesimwop, A. Lacombe priest o.m.i. (page 1)

Mistatimakabow, Sophie: B-136, Sophie Mistatimakabow, baptized 8 August 1863, age over one year, daughter of Mistatimakabow and [..], Godfather: Bazile Hammelin, Godmother: Louise Crise, Alb. Lacombe priest o.m.i. (page 49)

Mistekamin, Francois: B-47, Francois Mistekamin, baptized 17 September 1858, age two years, son of Mistekamin and Minowokapow, Godmother: Kipwatisiwop, A. Lacombe priest o.m.i. (page 6)

Mistikaskikus, Joseph: B-9, Joseph Mistikaskikus, baptized 22 June 1873, age 10 days, son of Mistikaskikus, infidel .., and Assimtestipiw..., Godmother: Angelique L☐Hirondelle, J. Joseph Dupuis priest o.m.i. (page 81)

Mittayik, Moise: B-16, Moise Mittayik, baptized 24 January 1859, age 20 days, son of Mittayik and Nancy Okimas, Godmother: Therese Akawat, A. Lacombe priest o.m.i. (page 11)

Miyaminowata, Sophia: B-16, Sophia Miyaminowata, baptized 11 January 1860, age 5 months, daughter of Miyaminowata and Katshikwetawakkionam, Godfather: Jean-Baptiste Courtepatte, Albert Lacombe priest o.m.i. (page 22)

Miyawayisuw, Louise: B-70, Louise Miyawayisuw, baptized 3 March 1861, age 16 months, daughter of Miyawayisuw and Josephte daughter of Omikis, Godmother: Angelique Batoche, Alb. Lacombe priest o.m.i. (page 32)

Mokkomitekkwe, Susanne: B-93, Susanne Mokkomitekkwe, baptized 10 November 1861, age 23 years, Godfather: Abraham Salois, Godmother: Therse Bisson, Alb. Lacombe priest o.m.i. (page 39)

Mongnon (Mondion), David: B-9, David Mongnon (Mondion), baptized 10 January 1860, age 6 months, son of Joseph Mongnon and Marianne, Godfather: Jean Baptiste Courtepatte, Godmother: Genevieve Loyer, Albert Lacombe priest o.m.i. (page 20)

Monroe/Munroe

Monroe, Antoine: B-14, Antoine Monroe, baptized 28 August 1884, son of Jenan Monroe and Sophie, Godmother: Bella Boucher, H. Grandin priest o.m.i. (page 100)

Monroe, Bella: B-11, Bella Monroe, baptized 5 August 1884, age 4 days, of the legitimate marriage of Jonas Monroe and Sophie K...., Godmother: Olive, H. Grandin priest. o.m.i. (page 99)

Monroe, Emelie: B-73, Emelie Monroe, baptized 15 March 1861, age 4 months, daughter of Felix Monroe and Louise Seguin dite Laderoute, Godfather: Olivier Seguin dit Laderoute, Godmother: Angelique L'Hyrondelle, J. M. St. Caer priest o.m.i. (page 33)

Monroe, Felix: B-35, Felix Monroe, baptized 25 July 1858, age 21 days, son of Felix Monroe and Louise Seguin Laderoute, Godmother: Angelique L'Hyrondelle, A. Lacombe priest o.m.i. (page 5)

Munroe, Sophie: B-4, Sophie Munroe, baptized 21 April 1872, age 6 months, Godmother: Catherine Cardinal, Godfather: J. Baptiste Hanasse [Vanasse], J. Joseph Dupuis priest o.m.i. (page 78)

St.Joachim, Fort Auguste (Fort Edmonton) 1858-1890

Montagnais, Louis and Marguerite Allary: M-2, Louis Montagnais, married 26 December 1870, Marguerite Allary, widow of Benjamin Vandale, Present: Pierre Deschenaux, A. Andre o.m.i. priest. (page 70)

Moreau, Charles: B-8, Charles Moreau, baptized 18 June 1873, age one month, son of Jonas Moreau and Cecile Desjarlais, Godfather: Charles Descheneaux, Godmother: Josette the wife of Pierre Descheneaux, the father was present, J. Joseph Dupuis priest o.m.i. (page 81)

Morin, Joseph: B-43, Joseph Morin, baptized 23 February 1861, age 2 weeks, son of Jean Baptiste Morin and Opimiskaw, Godfather: Louis Piche, Alb. Lacombe priest o.m.i. (page 28)

Morin, Pierre: B-12, Pierre Morin, baptized 11 January 1860, age 3 weeks, son of Jean-Baptiste Morin and Iyatwewitam, Godfather: Pierre Blandion, Albert Lacombe priest o.m.i. (page 21)

Morisset, Betsey: B-36, Betsey Morisset, baptized 10 January 1861, daughter of Norbert Morisset and Betsey Branconier, Godfather: Louis Kalliou, Godmother: Rosalie Goin, Alb. Lacombe priest o.m.i. (page 26)

Myers, Christine Mathilda: See Madison Barker and Christine Mathilda Myers

Nabesis, Josephte: B-13, Josephte Nabesis, baptized 1 August 1886, born yesterday, of the legitimate marriage of Baptiste Nabesis and Peggy, Godmother: Josette, H. Grandin o.m.i. (page 112)

Nabeses, Louisa: Louisa Nabeses, March 1885 confirmation, H. Grandin o.m.i. (page 104)

Nabessis, Pierre and Louisa: M-18, Pierre Nabessis, married 19 November 1884, Louisa, Present: Antoine Paquette and .. Mawinawata, H. Grandin priest o.m.i. (page 100)

Nabetih, Marie: B-141, Marie Nabetih, baptized 17 August 1863, age 6 months, son of Nabetih and Marguerite Piyeto, Godfather: Joseph Roy, Godmother: Henriette Cayen, Alb. Lacombe priest o.m.i. (page 50)

Nakaweywiw, Jean-Baptiste and Josephte: M-2, Jean-Baptiste Nakaweywiw, son of the late Antoine and Marie, married 27 January 1885, Josephte, minor daughter of Aiskuayiu and Josette Sokwew, Present: Louis Chartella and Peter Achorb, H. Grandin o.m.i. (page 103)

Nakaweyiniw, Johny: B-9, Johny Nakaweyiniw, baptized 10 June 1888, born _ June, of Jean-Baptiste Nakaweyiniw and Josette Amosiew [?], Godmother: Isabelle Mawtsksik, H. Grandin o.m.i. (page 125)

Nakkawayis, Rosalie: B-60, Rosalie Nakkawayis, baptized 1 March 1861, born today, daughter of Nakkawayis and Angelique Crise, Godfather: Alexis Cardinal, Alb. Lacombe priest o.m.i. (page 31)

St.Joachim, Fort Auguste (Fort Edmonton) 1858-1890

Namatis, Victoire: B-34, Victoire Namatis, baptized 7 September 1859, born yesterday, legitimate daughter of Ignace Namatis and Marguerite Beaudry, Godfather: Gabriel Dumont, Godmother: Suzanne Lucier, C. M. Frain m.o.m.i. (page 15)

Napessis, Alexandre: B-3, Alexandre Napesis, baptized 20 June 1870, born 4 June, of the legitimate marriage of William Napesis and Suzanne Pouilliac, Godmother: Louise Laurance, V. Tourmond priest. (page 69)

Naskipitun, Louis: B-4, Louis Naskipitun, baptized 11 February 1883, age 2 weeks, son of Jane Naskipitun, Godmother: Lucy, wife of Kipin, C. Scollen priest o.m.i. (page 87)

Neyiwatasiw, Joseph: B-15, Joseph Neyiwatasiw, baptized 3 February 1858, age 4 months, son of Jean Marie Neyiwatasiw and Marie Ganaweyim, Godmother: Rosalie Labonne, A. Lacombe priest o.m.i. (page 3)

Nipissing, Mary Jeanne: B-39, Mary Jeanne Nipissing, baptized 27 January 1861, at Fort de la Montagne, age 3 months, daughter of Michel Nipissing and Eloiza (Genevieve) Loyer, Godfather: Jean Baptiste Bruneau, Godmother: Cecile Lemire, Alb. Lacombe priest o.m.i. (page 27)

Nizodet, Thomas Gross-Tete: B-1, Thomas Nizodet Gross-Tete, baptized 11 May 1874, age 3 days, of the legitimate marriage of Antoine Nizodet a Gross-Tete and Catherine his wife, Godfather: Eustach Berard, Godmother: Marguerite his wife, J. Joseph Dupuis priest o.m.i. (page 82)

Nittawikwa, Pierre and Angelique Kistenaham: M-2, Pierre Nittawikwa, married 29 June 1865, Angelique Kistenaham, Present: Samuel Cunningham (signed) and Angelique L'Hyrondelle, Alb. Lacombe priest o.m.i. (page 60)

Norris, Anne: B-17, Anne Norris, baptized 5 June 1883, age one day, daughter of John Norris and Mary Kayatowew, Godfather: James Norris, C. Scollen priest o.m.i. (page 91)

Norris, Clara: B-14, Clara Norris, baptized 10 August 1886, age 10 days, daughter of Annie Inkster and James Norris, Godmother: Marie, wife of Norris, H. Grandin o.m.i., Z. Lizee priest o.m.i. (page 112)

Norris, James and Annie Inkster: M-5, James Norris (signed), legitimate adult son of John Norris and Marie __, married 20 September 1886, Annie Inkster, minor daughter of Robert Inkster and Harriet Anderson, Present: Louis Chastellain (signed) and A. A. Ringuette (signed), H. Grandin o.m.i. (page 116)

Norris, Jane Mary: B-17, Jane Mary Norris, baptized 28 December 1889, age 3 months, legitimate marriage of James Norris and Anna Inkster, Godfather: Jeremie Gladu, Godmother: Angelique Chalifou, V. Vegreville o.m.i. (page 133)

St.Joachim, Fort Auguste (Fort Edmonton) 1858-1890

Norris, Robert: B-15, Robert Norris, baptized 18 October 1887, age 5 weeks, son of Jammy Norris and Annie Inkster, Godmother: Clara Norris (signed), H. Grandin o.m.i. (married 23 October 1917 at Fort McMurray Christina Biggs, daughter of William Biggs and Helene Koka.) (page 121)

O☐Sawemustus, Moise: B-25, Moise O'Sawemustus, baptized 10 August 1883, age one month, son of O'Sawemustus and Iskwetew, Godfather: Mathias Colin, Godmother: Catherine Ayaimhagan, H. J. H. Blais priest o.m.i. (page 92)

O☐Saweyimase, Louis Napoleon: B-12, Louis Napoleon O'Saweyimase, baptized 3 April 1883, age 5 days, son of Francois O'Saweyimase and Isabelle Kanuste-Kwew, Godfather: Jos. Charretier, Godmother: Philomene, wife of Johnny Paul, C. Scollen priest o.m.i. (page 89)

Oapato, Marguerite: B-34, Marguerite Oapato, baptized 6 September 1860, age 4 months [parents unnamed], Godmother: Julia Papain, J. M. St.Caer o.m.i. (page 25)

Okimanasis, Marie: B-43, Marie Anne Okimanasis, baptized 1 October 1859, age 4 months, daughter of Alexis Okimanasis and Katshiskwe, Godfather: George Hatson, Godmother: Angelique L'Hyrondelle, Albert Lacombe priest o.m.i. (page 16)

Okimas, Alexandre, Henri and Benjamin: B-13, 14, 15, Alexandre, Henri and Benjamin Okimas, baptized 24 January 1859, Alexandre age 6 months, Henri age 2 years, Benjamin age one year, sons of Okimas and Opinakkwat, Godmother: Therese Akawas, A. Lacombe priest o.m.i. (page 11)

Okimawawaw, Betsy: B-9, Betsy Okimawawaw, baptized 30 May 1886, age 3 years, daughter of Alexandre Okimawawaw and Catherine, Godmother: Marie Anne Mamiwawataw, H. Grandin o.m.i. (page 111)

Okyiko, Jean Baptiste: B-14, Jean Baptiste Okyiko, baptized 11 January 1860, age 10 months, son of Okyiko and Nakawiskwe, Godfather: Pierre Blandion, Albert Lacombe priest o.m.i. (page 21)

Okyiko, Paul: B-20, Paul Okyiko, baptized 26 January 1859, age 2 years, son of Okyiko and Marie Okimas, Godfather: Joseph Kaminawan, Godmother: Louise Cardinal, A. Lacombe priest o.m.i. (page 11)

Omaskawisis, Michel: B-19, Michel Omaskawisis, baptized 3 February 1858, age 5 years, son of Omaskawisis and Kakikeyasit, Godfather: Michel Ayutshon, A. Lacombe priest o.m.i. (page 3)

Ominawatchakwe, Antoine: B-135, Antoine Ominawatchakwe, baptized 8 August 1863, age one month, son of Antoine Ominawatchakwe and Judith Belanger, Godfather: Edouard Genereux, Godmother: Marie Chatelain, Alb. Lacombe priest o.m.i. (page 48-49)

Onigotesis, Charles and Isabelle Courteoreille: M-3, Charles Onigotesis, minor son of Onigotesis, married 15 October 1865, Isabelle Courteoreille, minor daughter of Michel Courteoreille and Marie Crise, the fathers and mothers, Alb. Lacombe priest o.m.i. (page 60-61)

Otawa, Rosalie: B-22, Rosalie Otawa, baptized 5 February 1858, age 7 months, daughter of Joseph Otawa and Marianne Mongnon, Godmother: Angelique Mongnon, A. Lacombe priest o.m.i. (page 3)

Otchekatay, Lisette and Marianne
B-108 and B-109, Lisette and Marianne Otchekatay, baptized 1 April 1862, twin daughters of Otchekatay and Wabawes, Godfather for both: Michel Cardinal, Alb. Lacombe priest o.m.i. (page 42)

Oteyaniy, Helene: B-1, Helene Oteyaniy, baptized 1 April 1865, age one month, daughter of Oteyaniy and Helene Ayutchow, Godmother: Rosalie L'Hyrondelle, Alb. Lacombe priest o.m.i. (page 59)

Otjebikkes, William: B-38, William Otjebikkes, baptized 12 September 1858, age 3 years, son of Otjebikkes and Josephte Crise, Godmother: Cecile Lemire, A. Lacombe priest o.m.i. (page 5)

Owiyawit, Antoine and Suzanne: M-3, Antoine Owiyawit, son of Owiyawit and Rosalie, married 9 July 1886, Suzanne, daughter of Jack and the late Angelique, Witnesses: Witnesses: Z. Lizee priest o.m.i. (signed) and Georges St.Cyr (signed), H. Grandin o.m.i. (page 112)

Papaldy, Caroline: B-12, Caroline Papaldy, baptized 29 July 1886, age 12 days, daughter of Francois Papaldy and Pauline, Godmother: Veronique Okisiwkis, H. Grandin o.m.i. (page 112)

Parisien, Alexandre: B-7 Alexandre Parisien, baptized 26 January 1871, born yesterday of the legitimate marriage of the deceased J. Bte. Parisien and Isabelle Deschamps; Godfather Pierre __; V. Bourgine priest. (page 73)

Parisien, Baptiste: B-11, Baptiste Parisien, baptized 15 April 1886, born in the eve, of the legtimate marriage of Baptiste Parisien and Isabelle Deschamp, Godfather: Baptiste Deschamp, Godmother: Isabelle Alary, A. Andre o.m.i. priest. (page 62)

Paquette/Paquet

Paquet, Elize: B-121, Elize Paquet, baptized 12 December 1862, age one day, daughter of Henri Paquet and Cecile Durand, Godfather: Alexandre Simpson, Godmother: Marie Goin, Alb. Lacombe priest o.m.i. (page 45)

Paquette, Isabelle: See Peter Donald and Isabelle Paquette

Paquette, Marguerite: B-32, Marguerite Paquette, baptized 28 August 1860, born 20 August, legtimate daughter of Henry Paquette and Cecile Dumond, Godfather: Pierre St. Sauveur, Godmother: Marguerite Desjarlais, J. M. St. Caer [?] o.m.i. (page 25)

Paquet, Marie: B-2, Marie Paquet, baptized 28 March 1869, age 2 months, daughter of Joseph Paquet and Cecile Bruneau, a legitimate marriage, Godfather: Daniel Paul, Godmother: Marie Paul, V. Bourgine priest. (page 66)

Paquette, Marie Rose: B-17, Marie Rose Paquette, baptized 7 December 1887, age 4 days, daughter of Louis Paquette and Julie Dagneau, Godfather: Elie Dagneau, Godmother: Madeleine ..., H. Grandin o.m.i. (page 122)

Paquet, Norbert: B-13, Norbert Paquet, baptized 8 April 1871, age 4 days, of the legitimate marriage of Henri Paquet and Cecile Dumont, Godfather: Olivier Bellerose, represented by Antoine Paquet, Godmother: Marie Philomene, A. Andre o.m.i. priest. (page 74)

Paquette, Octave: B-16, Octave Paquette, baptized 6 September 1885, age 4 days, son of Louis Paquette and Julie Dagneau, Godfather: David Dagneau, Godmother: Julie Lawrence, H. Grandin o.m.i. (page 106)

Pasquette, Virginie: B-11, Virginie Pasquette, baptized 2 August 1873, son of Henri Pasquet and Cecile his wife, Godfather: Augustin Berard, Godmother: Helene wife of Collen [?], J. Joseph Dupuis priest o.m.i. (page 81-82)

Pattenaude, Marianne: See Francois Larocque and Marianne Pattenaude

Paul/Paulette/Pol

Pol, Betzy: B-4, Betzy Pol, baptized 11 May 1874, age 6 months, of the legitimate marriage of Johnny Pol and Marie Philomene Pasquet, Godfather: Henri Pasquet, Godmother: Angelique Sauve, J. Joseph Dupuis priest o.m.i. (page 83)

Paul, Daniel and Marguerite Deschamps: M-4, Daniel Paul, minor son of the deceased Paulet Paul, married 29 April 1869, Marguerite Deschamps, minor daughter of Francois Deschamps and Marguerite Canada, Present: H. Leduc, Alb. Lacombe priest o.m.i. (page 67)

Paul, Flora: B-7, Flora Paul, baptized 1 June 1890, born .., of Joseph Paul and Marie, Godfather: J. Baptiste Deschamps (Rabaska), Godmother: Marie Rose Dagnon, L. Fourquet priest. (page 137)

Paul, Flora Eliza: B-24, Flora Eliza Paul, baptized 31 October 1886, age 6 days, legitimate daughter of Joseph Paul and Agathe __, Godmother: Helene Beauregard, H. Grandin o.m.i. (page 117)

Paulette, Isabelle: B-1, Isabelle Paulette, baptized 13 May 1870, age about 3 months, of the legitimate marriage of Daniel Paulette and Marguerite Deschamps, Godfather: Francois Deschamps, Godmother: Louise Watemas, H. LeDuc priest o.m.i. (page 69)

Paul, John: B-3, John Paul, baptized 24 June 1865, age 8 days, son of John Paul and Philomene Paquet, Godfather: John Hatson (Signed John Hudson [written Hugdson with the "g" crossed out]), Godmother: Olive Bellerose, Alb. Lacombe priest o.m.i. (page 59)

Paul, Joseph: B-27, Joseph Paul, baptized 22 September 1883, age 10 days, of the legitimate marriage of John Paul and Philomene Paquette, Godfather: Paul Gibeau, Godmother: Julie MacDala, A. Fabre o.m.i. (page 93)

Paulette, Marianne: B-2, Marianne Paulette, baptized 15 May 1870, age 3 weeks, of the legitimate marriage of Johny Paulette and Philomene Paquette, Godfather: Edouard St.Sauveur, Godmother: Elise Cameron, H. LeDuc priest o.m.i. (page 69)

Paul, Marie: See Andrew Flett and Marie Paul

Paul, Marie-Anne: See Joe Bird and Marie-Anne Paul

Paul, Marie-Catherine: B-3, Marie-Catherine Paul, baptized 27 March 1887, age 15 days, daughter of Philomene Paquette and Johny Paul, Godfather: Thomas Berard, Godmother: Bella Berard, H. Grandin o.m.i. (page 119)

Paul, Nancy: B-3, Nancy Paul, baptized 31 December 1867, born 24 December, of the legitimate marriage of John Paul and Philomene Paquette, Godmother: Genevieve Paquette, H. Leduc priest o.m.i. (page 63)

Petit-Couteau, Moise and Marie Ayamihayan: M-7, Moise Petit-Couteau, adult son of Moise Petit-Couteau and the deceased Marie Blandion, married 24 November 1885, Marie Ayamihayan, minor daughter of Ayamihayan and Suzanne, Present: Otohikamis and f. Bilodeau, H. Grandin omi. (page 109)

Piche, Isabelle: B-21, Isabelle Piche, baptized 5 February 1858, age one year, daughter of Jean Baptiste Piche and Rosalie [Blandoin crossed out] Dion, Godfather: Pierre Blandion, A. Lacombe priest o.m.i. (page 3)

Piche, Louis: B-17, Louis Piche, baptized 24 January 1859, age 10 months, son of Louis Piche and Kiskikut, Godmother: Catherine Peketiw, A. Lacombe priest o.m.i. (page 11)

Piche, Marianne: B-8, Marianne Piche, baptized 2 February 1858, age 3 years, son of Louis Piche and Keskskm, Godmother: Sophie, wife of Piyssimwop, A. Lacombe priest o.m.i. (page 2)

Piche, Marie: B-9, Marie Piche, baptized 2 February 1858, age one year, daughter of Alexis Piche and Kasakotshimat, Godfather: Augustin Auger, Godmother: Rosalie Labonne, A. Lacombe priest o.m.i. (page 2)

Piche, Mathias: B-51, Mathias Piche, baptized 26 February 1861, age 5 months, son of Louis Piche and Kiskikut, Godfather: Jean L'Heureux, Alb. Lacombe priest o.m.i. (page 29)

Piche, Nancy: B-52, Nancy Piche, baptized 26 February 1861, age 5 months, daughter of Jean Baptiste Piche and Iskwatam, Godfather: Thomas Boucher, Alb. Lacombe priest o.m.i. (page 29)

Piche, Sophie: B-10, Sophie Piche, baptized 2 February 1858, age 4 months, daughter of Wabiskaskawan Piche and Kwatem [?], Godfather: Augustin Auger, A. Lacombe priest o.m.i. (page 2)

Piche, Susanne: B-9, Susanne Piche, baptized 24 January 1859, age 2 months, daughter of Alexys Piche and Kasekotshimat, Godmother: Otayamiwis, A. Lacombe priest o.m.i. (page 10)

Pied-noir, Marguerite: B-140, Marguerite Pied-noir, baptized 17 August 1863, age 2 years, daughter of Pied-noir and Ema Kaiamikkwewkwasok [?], Godmother: Marguerite Lalonde, Alb. Lacombe priest o.m.i. (page 49-50)

Pied-noir, Marie: B-120, Marie of the Pied-noirs, baptized 5 December 1862, age one year, Godfather: Felix Monroe, Alb. Lacombe priest o.m.i. (page 45)

Pikwatus, Marie: B-29, Marie Pikwatus, baptized 14 October 1883 age one year, of the marriage of Abraham Pikwatus and Marie, H. Grandin priest o.m.i. (page 93)

Pisimweyabiy, Susanne: B-23, Susanne Pisimweyabiy, baptized 30 January 1859, age about 60 years, Godfather: Louis Loyer, A. Lacombe priest o.m.i. (page 12)

Pittukahan, Marie: B-2, Marie Pittukahan, baptized 2 January 1859, age 6 years, daughter of Pittukahan, Godfather: Jean Baptiste Kalliou, Godmother: Louise Lucier, A. Lacombe priest o.m.i. (page 9)

Piwapiskokapaw, Isabelle: B-30, Isabelle Piwapiskokapaw, baptized 9 May 1858, age 3 months, daughter of Joseph Piwapiskokapaw and Piyesimwop, Godmother: Cecile, M. R. Remas p.o.m.i. (page 4)

Piycimwop, Albert: B-83, Albert Piycimwop, baptized 28 July 1861, age 7 days, son of Bruno Piycimwop and Sophie Larocque, Godfather: Louis Roussel, Godmother: Marie Decoignes, Alb. Lacombe priest o.m.i. (page 35)

Piyesimpwop, Peggy: B-4, Peggy Piyesimwop, baptized 25 April 1868, born 19 April, of the legitimate marriage of Moyse Piyesimwop and Marie Dion Wabiskay, Godfather: John McDougall (signed J. G. McDougald), Godmother: Olive Bellerose, H. Leduc priest o.m.i. (page 64)

Piyeto, Pierre: B-12, Pierre Piyeto, baptized 24 January 1859, age 10 months, son of Piyeto and Louise

Cardinal, Godmother: Atayamiwis, A. Lacombe priest o.m.i. (page 10)

Piyetweweham, Andre: B-20, Andre Piyetweweham, baptized 4 February 1858, age 3 months, son of Piyetweweham and Kakawipekinam, Godmother: Genevieve Mangnon, A. Lacombe priest o.m.i. (page 3)

Piyokakabew, Simon: B-11, Simon Piyokikabew, baptized 24 January 1859, age 11 months, son of Piyokikabew and Isabelle Piche, Godfather: Alexys Piche, A. Lacombe priest o.m.i. (page 10)

Piysimwap, Louis: B-71, Louis Piysimwap, baptized 7 March 1861, age 2 months, son of Michel Piysimwap and Julie Bisson, Godfather: Alexandre Savard, Godmother: Therese Bisson, J. M. St. Caer priest o.m.i. (page 33)

Primeau, Catherine: B-16, Catherine Primeau, baptized 1 September 1886, born 28 August 1886, of the legitimate marriage of Alexis Primeau and Annie Deschamps, Godfather: Joseph Deschamps, Godmother: Catherine Jeanne Fayan, H. Grandin o.m.i. (page 115)

Quinn, Abraham and his wife Marianne: Abraham Quinn and his wife Marianne of St.Albert, Papastches reserve, Riviere de terre Blanche were confirmed on 2 March 1884, Const. Scollen priest o.m.i. (page 97)

Quinn, Charles and his wife Jane: Charles Quinn and his wife Jane of St.Albert, Papastches reserve, Riviere de terre Blanche were confirmed on 2 March 1884, Const. Scollen priest o.m.i. (page 97)

Quinn, Clara: B-27, Clara Quinn, baptized 28 November 1886, age one month, legitimate daughter of Francois Quinn and Angelique, Godmother: Nancy Meaver, H. Grandin o.m.i. (page 118)

Quinn, Edward and his wife Sophie: Edward Quinn and his wife Sophie of St.Albert, Papastches reserve, Riviere de terre Blanche were confirmed on 2 March 1884, Const. Scollen priest o.m.i. (page 97)

Quinn, Eliza: B-13, Eliza Quinn, baptized 12 July 1885, born the 5th, of the legitimate marriage of Edward Quinn and Sophie, Godfather: Francis Nabesis, Godmother: Eliza Shields, H. Grandin o.m.i. (page 106)

Quinn, Frederic: B-17, Frederic Quinn, baptized 20 November 1884, age 8 days, legitimate son of Charles Quinn and Jeannie Thomas, Godfather: Frederic Durocher, Godmother: Veronique Guinn, Gabillon priest o.m.i. (page 101)

Quinn, Georges and his wife Anne: Georges Quinn and his wife Anne of St.Albert, Papastches reserve, Riviere de terre Blanche were confirmed on 2 March 1884, Const. Scollen priest o.m.i. (page 97)

Quinn, Georges: B-7, Georges Quinn, baptized 1 April 1885, age 5 months, son of William Quinn and

Helene, Godfather: Charles Quinn, Godmother: Jane, his wife, V. Gabillon priest o.m.i. (page 105)

Quinn, Isabelle: B-5, Isabelle Quinn, baptized 21 March 1885, age 4 months, daughter of Georges Quinn and Annie, Godfather: Tabatchiyin, Godmother: Pauline his wife, C. Scollen priest o.m.i. (page 104)

Quinn alias Gladu, Joe and Isabelle Gladu: M-2, Joe Quinn alias Gladu (x), son of Johny Quinn and Pagne Brenon [Peggie Bruneau], married 2 April 1890, Isabelle, daughter of Norwegian Gladu, Present: John Quinn (father of Joe) and Henry Laroque, L. Fouquet priest. (page 134)

Quinn, John: B-14, John Quinn, baptized 9 October 1887, age 5 [?] days, son of Edward Quinn and Sophie .., Godfather: Henry Munroe, Godmother: Eliza Shields, H. Grandin o.m.i. (page 121)

Quinn, Johny: B-4, Johny Quinn, baptized 31 March 1889, age 11 days, legitimate son of Edouard Quinn and Sophia, Godfather: Joseph Quinn, Godmother: Mrs. Irwin, H. Grandin o.m.i. (page 129)

Quinn alias Gladu, Johny and Cecile: M-1, Johny Quinn alias Gladu, widower of Julie Tom, married 2 April 1890, Cecile, widow of J. Baptiste Lanore, resident of Edmonton, Present: Jo. Quinn, Chs. Gladu Jr., and Henri Laroque, L. Fouquet priest. (page 134)

Quinn, Joseph: B-6, Joseph Quinn, baptized 17 April 1889, age ..., son of George Quinn and Annie, H. Grandin o.m.i. (page 129-130)

Quinn, Marie: B-6, Marie Quinn, baptized 8 May 1887, age 2 months, daughter of William Quinn (Iakulds) and Helene, Godfather: Francois Quinn, H. Grandin o.m.i. (page 119)

Quinn, Marie and William: B-22 and B-23, Marie and William Quinn, baptized 6 November 1885, Marie, age 2 months, daughter of William Quinn and Emma, Godmother: Jane Quinn, William age 2 months, son of Johny Quinn and Apicikwew, Godmother: Flora Quinn, H. Grandin omi. (page 108)

Quinn, Pauline: See Francois Tabatchiysis and Pauline Quinn

Quinn, St. Pierre: B-14, St. Pierre Quinn, baptized 1 September 1885, age 2 months, son of Johny Quinn dit Pie de Bois and Marguerite, Godmother: Maggy Young alias Mac Kenny, H. Grandin o.m.i. (page 106)

Rabaska, Alexandre: B-22, Alexandre Rabaska, baptized 13 October 1886, born 11 October 1886, of the legitimate marriage of Joseph Rabaska and Therese Dagneau, Godfather: Louis Paquette, Godmother: Julie Dagneau, Z. Lizee priest o.m.i. (page 117)

Rabaska, Anastasie: B-19, Anastasie Rabaska, baptized 19 September 1886, age 8 days, daughter of Jean Baptiste Rabaska and Marguerite Berard, Godfather: Lawrence Garneau, Godmother: Helene Beauregard, H. Grandin o.m.i. (page 115)

Rabaska, Jerrey: B-2, Jerrey (Rabaska), baptized 10 February 1885, age 9 days, son of Nancy Rabaska, father unknown, Godmother: Nancy, H. Grandin o.m.i. (page 103)

Racette, Victoire: See Francois Bruneau and Victoire Racette

Raymond, Daniel: B-5, Daniel Raymond, baptized 10 May 1873, born this morning, son of Roger Raymond ... and Elisabeth Bruno, his wife, Godfather: Augustin Berard, Godmother: ..., J. Joseph Dupuis priest o.m.i. (page 80)

Richard, Moise: B-55, Moise Richard, baptized 13 December 1858, age 2 months, son of James Richard and Judith Godin, Godfather: James Short, Godmother: Angelique Maskatelwan, A. Lacombe priest o.m.i. (page 7)

Robertson, Magloire: B-166, Magloire Robertson, baptized 2 October 1864, born yesterday, son of Jean Baptiste Robertson and Marguerite Auger, Godfather: Thomas Kalliou, Godmother: Marie Josi [Finley ?], Alb. Lacombe priest o.m.i. (page 56)

Roussel, Andre: B-96, Andre Roussel, baptized 4 February 1862, born 31 January, son of Louis Roussel and Angelique Tessier, Godfather: Pierre Dumont, Godmother: Susanne Bouvet, Alb. Lacombe priest o.m.i. (page 40)

Roussel, Angelique: B-27, Angelique Roussel, baptized 23 March 1858 age 14 days, daughter of Louis Roussel and Angelique Tessier, Godfather: Jean Baptiste Faynand [?], A. Lacombe priest o.m.i. (page 4)

Roussel, John: B-167, John Roussel, baptized 22 October 1864, born 20 October, son of Louis Roussel and Angelique Tessier, Godfather: Samuel Cunningham (signed), Godmother: Marguerite Brazeau, M. A. Remas priest o.m.i. (page 56)

Roussel, Louis: B-26, Louis Roussel, baptized 1 February 1860, born today, of Louis Roussel and Angelique Tessier, Godfather: Antoine Gouin, Godmother: Marie Rolland, C. M. Frain p.o.m.i. (page 23)

Rowland/Rowlland/Roland

Rowlland, Agnes: B-7, Agnes Rowlland, baptized 9 May 1887, age 26 days, daughter of Julie Moar and Jammy Rowlland, Godfather: C. Thiriault, H. Grandin o.m.i. (page 120)

Rowlland, Amelia: B-15, Amelia Rowlland, baptized 16 September 1884, age 6 months, daughter of Jemmy Rowlland and Julie Mac Gillis, Godmother: Betsy Rowlland, H. Grandin priest o.m.i. (page 100)

St.Joachim, Fort Auguste (Fort Edmonton) 1858-1890

Rowland, Betsey: B-56, Betsey Rowland, baptized 15 December 1858, age 4 days, daughter of William Rowland and Helene Beauregard, Godfather: Alexandre Savard, Godmother: Marguerite Bisson, A. Lacombe priest o.m.i. (page 8)

Roland, Johny: B-1, Johny Roland, baptized 6 January 1872, born this morning, son of William Roland, protestant, and Helene Beauregard, catholic, Godfather: Henri Paquette, Godmother: Cecile Dumont, Joseph Dupuis priest o.m.i. (page 76)

Saint-Clair, David: B-32, David Saint-Clair, baptized 18 May 1859, age 35 years, 3 months, Godfather: Abraham Salois, Godmother: Suzanne Bouvet, C. M. Frain m.o.m.i. (page 13)

Saint-Clair, David and Marie McDonald: M-5, David Saint-Clair, adult son of Baki St.Clair and Elisabeth Swan, married 19 May 1859, Marie McDonald, minor daughter of Mordo McDonald and Louise Bouvet, Present: Joseph Ward, Louis Larence and Abraham Saluam [Salois], C. M. Frain priest. (page 14)

Saint Sauveur/St.Sauveur

St.Sauveur, Joseph: B-1, Joseph St.Sauveur, baptized 27 January 1867, born 17 January, of the legitimate marriage of Pierre St.Sauveur and Marie Gouin, Godfather: Joseph Benoit, Godmother: Marguerite Savard, A. Andre priest o.m.i. (page 63)

St.Sauveur, Samuel: B-35, Samuel St.Sauveur, baptized 9 December 1860, born today, son of Pierre St.Sauveur and Marie Goin, Godfather: John Cunningham (signed), Godmother: Catherine Bruneault, Alb. Lacombe priest o.m.i. (page 26)

Saint Sauveur, Sophie: B-111, Sophie Saint Sauveur, baptized 15 September 1862, born today, daughter of Pierre St.Sauveur and Marie Goin, Godfather: Jean Baptiste Courtepatte, Godmother: Josephte Bellecourt, Alb. Lacombe priest o.m.i. (page 43)

(Salois) Salouen, Louis: B-30, Louis Salouen (Salois), baptized 8 May 1860, age 4 months 5 days, legtimate son of Abraham Salouen and Suzanne Bouvet, Godfather: Louis Larence, Godmother: Marguerite Brazeau, C. M. Frain o.m.i. (page 24)

Salois, Salomon: B-162, Salomon Salois, baptized 3 September 1864, age 15 days, son of Abraham Salois and susanne Beauvais, Godfather: Xavier Plante, Godmother: Marguerite Brazeau, Alb. Lacombe priest o.m.i. (page 55)

Savard, Alexandre and Therese Bisson: M-1, Alexandre Savard, married 1 January 1858, Therese Bisson, Present: Antoine Galarneau and Jean Baptiste Bisson, A. Lacombe priest o.m.i. (page 1)

Savard, Bella: B-2, Bella Savard, baptized 17 January 1869, born [..], legitimate daughter of Antoine Savard and Marguerite Bisson, Godfather: Magloire Grey, Godmother: Catherine Bellerose, V. Bourgine priest. (page 66)

Savard, Eloiza: B-150, Eloiza Savard, baptized 5 September 1863, age 6 days, daughter of Antoine Savard and Marguerite Bisson, Godfather: George Hudson, Godmother: Mary Roland, Alb. Lacombe priest o.m.i. (page 52)

Savard, John: B-90, John Savard, baptized 14 October 1861, born yesterday, son of Alexandre Savard and Therese Bisson, Godfather: Samuel Cunningham, Godmother: Rosalie L'Hyrondelle, J. M. Caer priest o.m.i. (page 37-38)

Savard, Octave: B-16, Octave Savard, baptized 14 October 1866, b. 10 October, of the legitimate marriage of Antoine Savard and Marguerite Bisson, Godfather: Octave Belrose, Godmother: Rosalie L'hirondelle, A. Andre o.m.i. priest. (page 62)

Savard, Philippe: B-82, Philippe Savard, baptized 10 July 1861, born yesterday, son of Antoine Savard and Marguerite Bisson, Godmother: Angelique L'Hyrondelle, Alb. Lacombe priest o.m.i. (page 35)

Savard, Therese: B-4, Therese Savard, baptized 22 January 1859, born day before yesterday, of Alexandre Savard and Therese Bisson, Godfather: Louis Larence, Godmother: Rosalie Labonne, C. M. Frain o.m.i. (page 9)

Sawan (Nepissing), Adelaide: B-26, Adelaide Sawan (Nepissing), baptized 30 March 1859, age over 2 months, legitimate daughter of Thomas Sawan and Rose Gladu, Godfather: Antoine Galarneau, Godmother: Rose Joduguine [?], C. M. Frain m.o.m.i. (page 12)

Sawan, Alexys: B-25, Alexys Sawan, baptized 5 February 1858, age one year, son of Sawan and Kawayokabawi, Godfather: Alexys Cardinal, A. Lacombe priest o.m.i. (page 4)

Sawan, Marguerite: B-69, Marguerite Sawan, baptized 3 March 1861, age 2 years, daughter of Sawan and Nawanokabawek, Godmother: Marguerite Hainault, Alb. Lacombe priest o.m.i. (page 32)

Sawan, Marie: B-24, Marie Sawan, baptized 5 February 1858, age 3 years, daughter of Sawan and Kawayokabawi, Godmother: Marianne Mongnon, A. Lacombe priest o.m.i. (page 4)

Shalifoux, Noel: B-2, Noel Shalifoux, baptized 8 January 1860, born today, son of Paul Shalifoux and Genevieve Campion, Godfather: Noel Courtepatte, Godmother: Nancy Campion, Albert Lacombe priest o.m.i. (page 19)

Shields, David Walter: B-18, David Walter Shields, baptized 18 November 1888, born 1 November 1888, of the legitimate marriage of John Shields and Eliza Anderson, Godfather: Henry Meaver, Godmother: Annie Bradshaw, H. Grandin o.m.i. (page 126)

Shields, Jenny Florence: B-10, Jenny Florence Shields, baptized 10 May 1885, age 17 days, legitimate daughter of John Shields and Eliza Anderson, and Maraia, age 19 days, daughter of Alexis and Isabelle .... of Florence Anne Mavor, Godmother: Maria M.. femme Norris, H. Grandin o.m.i. (page 105)

Shields, John and Elisa Anderson: M-10, John Shields (signed John W. Shields), adult son of David Shields and Margaret Waloby, married 1 July 1884, Elisa [Anderson], daughter of Jane Gladu and Alexandre Anderson, Witnesses: F. H. Bradshaw (signed) and John Foisy (signed), H. Grandin priest o.m.i. (page 99)

Short, Daniel: B-114, Daniel Short, baptized 11 May 1862, age 3 months, son of James Short and Angelique Maskistebwan, Godfather: Alexandre Landry, Godmother: Catherine Parent, Alb. Lacombe priest o.m.i. (page 43)

Simakanis (Rowand), Angelique: B-8, Angelique Simakanis Rowand, baptized 1 April 1885, age 2 months, daughter of Pierre Simakanis and Elise, Godfather: Abraham __, Godmother: Genevieve, his wife, V. Gabillion priest o.m.i. (page 105)

Simakanis, Betsy: B-14, Betsy Simakanis, baptized 9 May 1883, age 3 weeks, daughter of Simakanis and Elise Wapestakay, Godfather: Pierre Gladu, Godmother: Ellene, wife of William Gladu, C. Scollen priest o.m.i. (page 90)

Sinclair, David: B-3, David Sinclair, baptized 21 March 1875 at Fort de la Montagne, age one year, legitimate son of David Sinclair and Marie McDonald, Godfather: Baptiste Dumond, Godmother: his wife, Donnald priest o.m.i. (page 86)

Sinclair, Susanne: B-38, Susanne Sinclair, baptized 27 January 1861 at Fort de la Montagne, age 5 months, daughter of David Sinclair and Marie McDonnell, Godfather: Charles Hammelin, Godmother: Susanne Bouvais, Alb. Lacombe priest o.m.i. (page 27)

Siyakask, Emma: B-17, Emma Siyakask, baptized 3 February 1858, age one year, daughter of Siyakask and Angelique Maskwapimuttet, Godfather: Pierre Labonne (Beaudoin), A. Lacombe priest o.m.i. (page 3)

Siyakask, Francois: B-6, Francois Siyakask, baptized 8 January 1860, age 6 months, son of Siyakask and Angelique Wakikut, Godmother: Marie Nepissing, Albert Lacombe priest o.m.i. (page 20)

Siyakask, Joseph: B-100, Joseph Siyakask, baptized 19 March 1862, age 3 months, son of Siakask and Angelique Wakikut, Godfather: Alexis Cardinal, Alb. Lacombe priest o.m.i. (page 41)

Siykimak, Pierre and Marie Anikanis: M-2 Pierre Siykimak, married .. May 1873, Marie Anikanis, Witnesses: Attenawe and Piyesemest, J. Joseph Dupuis priest o.m.i. (page 80)

St.Joachim, Fort Auguste (Fort Edmonton) 1858-1890

Smith, Louis: B-137, Louis Smith, baptized 17 August 1863, age 3 months, son of Joseph Smith dit Laferte and Raciweyane, Godmother: Sophie Chatelain, Alb. Lacombe priest o.m.i. (page 49)

Soulier, Alexys: B-1, Alexys Soulier, baptized 1 January 1859, born today, son of George Soulier and Marie Kowikew, Godfather: Jean Baptiste Maskutebwan, Godmother: Rose Wanatch, A. Lacombe priest o.m.i. (page 9)

St.Arnault, Louis and ...: M-2, Louis St.Arnault [.....] married 10 May 1858, [...]. (page 4)

Stoney, Marie: B-5, Marie Stoney, baptized 20 August 1865, age one month, daughter of Stoney and Marie Kisiwatisiw, Godmother: Jane Collin, J. Tisiot priest o.m.i. (page 60)

Tabatchiysis, Francois and Pauline Quinn: M-4, Francois Tabatchiysis, married 21 March 1885, Pauline Quinn, Witness: Georges Quinn, C. Scollen priest o.m.i. (page 104)

Tabatchiysis, Paul: B-21, Paul Tabatchiysis, baptized 23 October 1884, age 6 months, son of Francois Tabatchiysis and Pauline Quinne, Godfather: Georges Quinne, Godmother: Annie, his wife, C. Scollen priest o.m.i. (page 101)

Takkutch, Benjamin: B-6, Benjamin Takkutch, baptized 13 September 1868, age 3 weeks, son of William Takkutch and Marguerite Mac, Godfather: Olivier Bellerose, Godmother: Clarisse Savard, Alb. Lacombe priest o.m.i. (page 65)

Tastawitch, Alexandre: B-48, Alexandre Tastawitch, baptized 27 February 1861, age 5 months, son of Tastawitch and Catherine Bruneau, Godfather: Alexis Okimanasis, Alb. Lacombe priest o.m.i. (page 29)

Tastawitch, Catherine: B-6, Catherine Tastawitch, baptized 31 January 1858, age 20 days, daughter of Tastawitch and Catherine Bruno, Godfather: Pierre Kisikawakapaw, Godmother: Catherine Sesesiw, A. Lacombe priest o.m.i. (page 1)

Tchipetakikwaneskwan, Edouard: B-6, Edouard Tchipetakikwaneskwan, baptized 1 April 1885, age .. weeks, son of Xavier Tchipetakikwaneskwan and Louisa Pepamikisikwew, Godfather: Edouard Quinn, Godmother: Elise Simakanis, V. Gabillon, priest o.m.i. (page 105)

Todd, Marie: See Pierre Boucher and Marie Todd

Tourangeau, Alex and La Louise Beaudry: M-11, Alex Tourangeau, son of unknown parents, married 2 August 1884, La Louise Beaudry, daughter of an unknown father and mother, Present: H. Grandin o.m.i., C. Scollen priest o.m.i. (page 99)

Tshakwapewis, Albert: B-165, Albert Tshakwapewis, baptized 5 September 1864, age [..], Godfather: Peter Andrew, M. R. Remas priest o.m.i. (page 55)

Vallee, Angelique: See Bazile Hebert and Angelique Vallee

Vanasse/Anas/Hanaze

[Vanasse], Adelaide Hanaze: B-5, Adelaide Hanaze [Vanasse], baptized 22 May 1874, age 3 months, of the legitimate marriage of J. Baptiste Hanaze and Catherine Cardinal, Godmother: Marguerite Marie Berard, J. Joseph Dupuis priest o.m.i. (page 83)

[Vanasse], Anas, Charles
B-78, Charles Anas [Vanasse], baptized 10 May 1861, age 7 days, son of Jean Baptiste Anas and Catherine Cardinal, Godfather: Olivier Seguin dit Laderoute, Godmother: Marie Comtois, M. R. Remas p.o.m.i. (page 34)

[Vanasse] Hanasse, Marie Catherine: B-6, Marie Catherine Hanasse [Vanasse], baptized 18 April 1872 at Fort la Montagne, age 11 days, legitimate daughter of Jean Baptiste Hanasse and Catherine Cardinal, his wife, Godfather: Joseph Allard, Godmother: Betsy Brazeau, J. J. Dupuis priest o.m.i. (page 77)

Vanasse, Philomene: See Jean Baptiste Dumont and Philomene Vanasse

Vandale, Adelaide: B-12, Adelaide Vandale, baptized 17 August 1884, born yesterday, of the legitmate marriage of Norman Vandale and Julie Monroe, Godfather: Maxime Eustache Ruset, H. Grandin o.m.i. (page 110)

Vandale, Magloire: B-16, Magloire Vandale, baptized 25 December 1889, age 4 days, of the legitimate marriage of Norman Vandale and Julie Monroe, Godfather: Magloire Robison, Godmother: Madeleine Cardinal, V. Vegreville o.m.i. (page 132)

Villebrun, Daniel and Catherine Patakokat: M-1, Daniel Villebrun (signed), married 22 May 1870, Catherine Patakokat, Witnesses: Olivier Bellerose (signed), Andre o.m.i priest. (page 69)

Wapuskaw, Alexis and Marie Kapawis: M-4, Alexis Wapuskaw, married 12 May 1872, Marie Kapawis, Witnesses: Henri Paquet Sr., Henry Paquet, Jr., Antoine Paquet, and Louis L'Hirondelle, J. Joseph Dupuis priest o.m.i. (page 78)

Wapuskaw, Joseph and Marie Ketiskwewin: M-1, Joseph Wapuskaw, married 7 January 1872, Marie Ketiskwewin, Witnesses: Isaac Dagneau, Francois Deschamps, and Eustache Berard, Joseph Dupuis priest o.m.i. (page 76-77)

Wapuskaw, Alexis: B-3, Alexis Wapuskaw, baptized 4 January 1872, age 6 days, son of Henri Wapuskaw and Susanne, Godmother: Nancy, wife of Moses, Joseph Dupuis priest o.m.i. (page 77)

Ward, Caroline: B-5, Caroline Ward, baptized 11 February 1883, age 7 days, daughter of William Ward and Therese Gladu, Godmother: Julie, wife of Dagnon, C. Scollen priest o.m.i. (page 87)

Ward, Georges: B-48, Georges Ward, baptized 18 December 1859, age one month, legitimate son of William Ward and Jeanne LaPatate, Godfather: Georges Hatson, Godmother: Marie Rolland, C. M. Frain m.o.m.i. (page 17)

Ward, Georges and Veronique Gladu: M-3, Georges Ward, adult son of William Ward and Jane Lapatac, married 4 October 1883, Veronique Gladu, minor daughter of Charles Gladu and Jane, Present: William Ward and Xavier Lapatac, C. Scollen priest o.m.i. (page 93)

Ward, John: B-36, John Ward, baptized 25 July 1858, age one month, son of James Ward and Catherine Bruno, Godfather: Jean Baptiste Bruno, Godmother: Cecile Tessier, A. Lacombe priest o.m.i. (page 5)

Ward, Louise: B-29, Louise Ward, baptized 8 May 1860, age one month, legitimate daughter of Peter Ward and Rosalie Bisson, Godfather: Felix Monereau [Monroe], Godmother: Louise Olivier [Laderoute], C. M. Frain o.m.i. (page 24)

Ward, Nancy: B-25, Nancy Ward, baptized 20 February 1859, age a few days, daughter of Catherine Ward, Godfather: Pierre Beauchamp, Godmother: Therese Bisson, A. Lacombe priest o.m.i. (page 12)

Ward, Nancy: See Pierre Beauchamp and Nancy Ward

Ward, Patrick: B-79, Patrick Ward, baptized 26 May 1861, born yesterday, son of James Ward and Catherine Bruno, Godfather: Antoine Gouin, Godmother: Jeaneve [..], Alb. Lacombe priest o.m.i. (page 34-35)

Wawas-Kesiw, Joseph: B-23, Joseph Wawas-Kesiw, baptized 5 August 1883, age 4 weeks, son of Wawas-Kesiw and Nancy, Godfather: Louis Laframboise, Godmother: Isabelle, his wife, H. J. H. Blais priest o.m.i. (page 92)

Wekimawiyam, Elizabeth: B-31, Elizabeth Wekimawiyam, baptized 10 May 1858, age 18 years, Godfather: Abraham Sallois, M. R. Remas p.o.m.i. (page 4)

Wetyiwiyim, Catherine: B-116, Catherine Wetyiwiyim, baptized 11 May 1862, age 2 years, daughter of Wetyiwiyim and Catherine Crise, Godmother: Catherine Parent, Alb. Lacombe priest o.m.i. (page 44)

Wikaskoseyim, Jean Baptiste: B-1, Jean Baptiste Wikaskoseyim, baptized 24 January 1871, born of Abraham Wikaskoseyim of Indian parents, Godfather: Baptiste Wallett, Godmother: Cecile Courchene, A. Andre o.m.i. priest. (page 72)

Wikaskoseyim, Josephine: B-5, Josephine Wikaskoseyim, bt, 24 January 1871, age 20 years, of Abraham Wikaskoseyim, Godfather: Reverend Father Andre o.m.i., Godmother: Josephine Courchaine, A. Andre o.m.i. priest. (page 72)

Wippuskaw, Caroline: B-15, Caroline Wipuskaw, baptized 19 October 1873, age 4 weeks, daughter of Alexis Wipuskaw and Marie Cabawis, Godmother: Marguerite Shalifau, Constantin Scollen priest o.m.i. (page 82)

Wipuskaw, Jean Baptiste and Sophie Osawiyamin: M-1, Jean Baptiste (Wipuskaw), adult son of Wipuskaw and Marie, married 10 January 1885, Sophie, minor daughter of Francois Osawiyamin and the deceased Sophie, Present: Wipuskaw and M. Gauvreau, H. Grandin p o.m.i. (page 103)

Wragge, Mary: See Louis Philipe Cazeau and Mary Wragge

****

B-15 crossed out version of B-16

[page 18 is tally sheet for 1859]

[page 57 is a copy of page 56]

B-30 and B-31 page 93 are illegible

B-1, page 95 is illegible

M-3, page 95 is illegible

B-2, page 96 is illegible

M-4, page 96 is illegible

[no page 114]

B-5 for 1888 is missing (page 124)

[no page 128]

www.ingramcontent.com/pod-product-compliance
Lightning Source LLC
Chambersburg PA
CBHW081114280526
45787CB00007B/2827